" *Once we had a planet. Now we're left with a suburb.* "

— **John Simpson in**
A Mad World, My Masters: Tales from a Traveller's Life

Contents

TAN WEE CHENG

EXOTIC LANDS

AND DODGY PLACES

ADVENTURES IN GREENLAND, THE AMAZON AND OTHER FAR-OUT PLACES

Parts of this book were previously published as *The Greenland Seal Hunter* by Times Editions.

© 2010 Marshall Cavendish International (Asia) Pte Ltd

Published by Marshall Cavendish Editions
An imprint of Marshall Cavendish International
1 New Industrial Road, Singapore 536196

Other Marshall Cavendish Offices

Marshall Cavendish Ltd. PO Box 65829, London EC1P 1NY, UK • Marshall Cavendish Corporation. 99 White Plains Road, Tarrytown NY 10591-9001, USA • Marshall Cavendish International (Thailand) Co Ltd. 253 Asoke, 12th Flr, Sukhumvit 21 Road, Klongtoey Nua, Wattana, Bangkok 10110, Thailand • Marshall Cavendish (Malaysia) Sdn Bhd, Times Subang, Lot 46, Subang Hi-Tech Industrial Park, Batu Tiga, 40000 Shah Alam, Selangor Darul Ehsan, Malaysia

Marshall Cavendish is a trademark of Times Publishing Limited

National Library Board, Singapore Cataloguing-in-Publication Data

Tan, Wee Cheng.
Exotic lands and dodgy places : adventures in Greenland, the Amazon and other far-out places / Tan Wee Cheng. — Singapore : Marshall Cavendish Editions, c2010.
p. cm.
ISBN : 978-981-4302-90-6 (pbk.)
1. Tan, Wee Cheng — Travel. 2. Voyages and travels. I. Title.
G465
910.4 — dc22   OCN672929846

Printed in Singapore by Fabulous Printers Pte Ltd

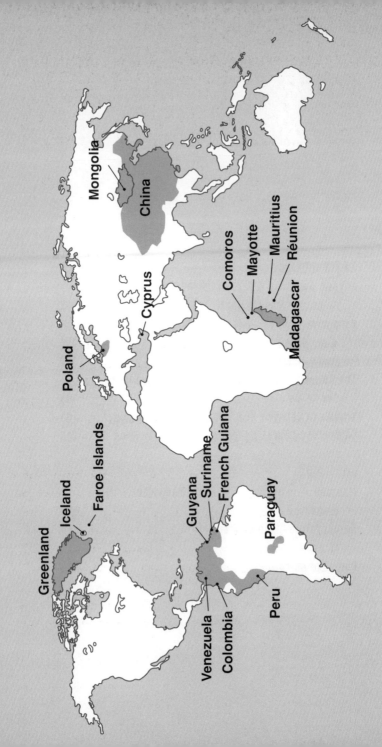

Introduction

When I was ten, Mother brought home a box of colourful stamps from the office. I remember that most of the stamps were still stuck onto the original envelopes. They fascinated me, not just the excitement of holding something from an exotic, faraway land, but also the very fact that these tiny objects had travelled a long way to reach my home. Later, Dad brought home a simple but colourful map of the world, with different colours representing different states. From then on, I became obsessed with exotic lands and their cultures.

I come from an ordinary Singapore family. Those were the days before budget airlines and mass tourism. Vacations usually meant a chalet weekend in Changi. For a long time I'd thought that my travels would be restricted to the armchair variety. Before long, I became an expert on trivial facts such as the old name of Burkina Faso, the whereabouts of some long-forgotten Paraguayan dictator and whether Greenland was green or white.

How the world has changed! After graduating from university, I decided to backpack around Western Europe against the advice of family and friends who felt that it was too dangerous to travel independently. I was bitten by the travel bug and the love of travelling became an incurable disease. The very sense of achievement after undertaking a major journey was intoxicating. One journey followed another: Eastern Europe, Middle East, China, Central Asia, the former USSR, Latin America, Africa and the Pacific.

In an increasingly globalised and capitalistic world, governments and businessmen have invested in tourism and transportation infrastructure to make it easy to travel. The availability of well-written guidebooks provides everyone with practical advice on even the most exotic and faraway countries. There are few places that are difficult or outrageously prohibitive in cost to reach for the average citizen of any developed country; whereas a mere hundred years ago, such journeys could only be undertaken as major expeditions by highly connected and extremely wealthy members of the elite.

While major international tourism cities once appealed to me, it soon dawned on me that I was attracted to places I knew little about, or places where I was least likely to bump into tourists on package holidays. Places that now get me excited are those which are more likely to be featured in National Geographic than Condé Nast Traveller, or hot spots that insurers would hesitate to cover.

I am neither a mountaineer nor a hardcore explorer. Climbing Mount Everest or braving the sandstorms of the Empty Quarter are not my cup of tea. I am more interested in simple journeys on public transport, albeit through epic routes like the Silk Road or the Trans-Siberian; or visiting places with strange names like Ouzarzate or Tierra del Fuego; or the recent battlefields of the Balkans and hotspots like Armenia and Azerbaijan, which — for someone interested in history, politics and economics — are particularly fascinating.

Even then, the places I have travelled to are not extraordinarily unusual. Many are standard destinations of slightly more adventurous backpackers from the United States, Europe and Australasia. Increasingly, I also bump into fellow Singaporeans in the most unexpected places, ranging from Azerbaijan to Mongolia and Colombia.

What I have included in this book represent an exotic sampling of my stories and encounters in a number of off-the-beaten-track areas, as well as impressions and thoughts about a few more familiar destinations. History, current affairs and business have always been my passions. My thoughts often evolve around the colourful coincidences of history and culture that I discover during my journeys, as well as the intricacies of development and the reasons for the lack of social and economic progress in certain countries.

This book is a revised edition of my 2004 book *The Greenland Seal*

Hunter. I have added photos and maps too so that my readers can travel with me visually through these distant lands. I have also included in this edition stories relating to my journeys to Mauritius, Venezuela, Guyana, Suriname and French Guiana.

There are many of you whom I should thank as you have helped me during my journeys, or made them more enjoyable. I had considered listing your names but have decided that the list would be nowhere close to being complete or fair. You know who you are, thank you very much! Lastly, I would like to dedicate this book to my family who have supported my never-ending wanderlust through their concern and advice.

Tan Wee Cheng
October 2010

THE NORTH ATLANTIC

Greenland is Ice and Iceland is Green (2001)

Greenlandic Seal Hunter for a Day

I had barely arrived at Mette's home when her telephone rang.

"Look here, Wee Cheng, there's going to be a seal hunt today. If you are interested, you must set off now."

I changed into the bulky outfit which Mette handed me — a multi-layered thick windbreaker, long johns and heavy boots which made me feel like a spaceman — and joined Benti on his weekend seal hunt.

Benti was 39 and a native Inuit Greenlander (previously known as Eskimos, but now considered a derogatory term due to its reference to people who eat raw meat), whose youthful face did not betray the many hours spent in the cold biting winds of this harsh frontier land. He worked at Kulusuk's only supermarket during the weekdays and hunted during the weekends for vital seal meat to feed his family and their 15 dogs. Dog sledges remain an important mode of transport in this remote part of Greenland and the dogs have to be well fed even in the summer months when the sledges are hardly used.

We hopped onto Benti's small, two-metre long wooden boat, which he had bought ten years ago in Tasiilaq. The Inuits of today no longer hunt on kayaks, a local invention known worldwide and one of the few Inuit words that have entered the English language. On Benti's boat were three rifles, a strange long stick with a hook at the end and a long steel harpoon somewhat worn out by age, plus a thermos flask of coffee made half an hour ago by Benti's wife, a few plastic cups and two packs of cookies — in case we stayed out at sea too long, said Benti. There were a few orange-coloured safety jackets as well. Benti smiled in a semi-defensive manner, "My sons were with me this morning, and they are young." Perhaps he felt the need to apologise for the presence of the safety jackets, which might have diminished the symbolism of Inuit manhood.

We sailed out of the harbour slowly, carefully negotiating the numerous icebergs that had drifted into the sound between Kulusuk Island and the Greenlandic mainland. Here, the mountains loomed high in the background, haunting greyish silhouettes, and these, as well as the floating icebergs and onshore glaciers, reflected light at every angle. A graceful minke whale followed us, while sea gulls circled above, hoping that we would net a delicious catch and allow them some leftovers. It was hard to believe that a mere 24 hours ago, I had been sitting in a bank in London, talking to clients about the risk of Forex fluctuations.

We navigated amongst ice slabs and drifting ice. No seals were seen in the first hour or so. Benti started to get impatient. Maybe his friends were wrong. They had seen numerous seals coming in with the southwards drifting ice. A boat had netted 17 for the day. A few motorboats sped past us and Benti waved to his friends — most of Kulusuk's residents were going to the largest town in the district, Tasiilaq, for the East Greenland Football Championships. His wife had wanted him to sail her there. "No way," he had told her, as the dogs needed to be fed.

Greenland: Icebergs everywhere, as far as the horizons.

Benti scanned the ice and water. "Seal! Seal!" He shouted suddenly. To me, there was nothing but icy waste all around. Well, one had to trust an Inuit in his natural environment; after all, these people had more than 30 words to describe ice. "Look at that moving black spot on the ice," he said, pointing at a location some hundred metres ahead.

We sailed closer and Benti switched off the engine. He loaded rounds of Maxi Mag 22 WMR — bought at the Kulusuk supermarket (DKK75 for a 50-round pack) — into his rifle, a Magnum Marlin bought at the Tasiilaq market for DKK3,000 (US$400). He rested the rifle on a handle, aimed at the black harp seal and pressed the trigger. Boom!

"Shit!" He shouted. He had missed, and the seal turned. He aimed, pressed the trigger and missed again. "This rifle needs zeroing," Benti shouted angrily. He needed to be quick, as the seal was wriggling its way towards the water. He hit it on his third attempt. It jerked, then laid still.

We sped towards the ice slab and there it was, bleeding profusely. Its warm blood had not only coloured its rich black coat red, but had also melted a hole through the ice. The blood had flowed through and began to turn the water a bloody red. Benti raised his harpoon, then thrust it through the seal's eye, dealing it a final blow. Only a courageous man could do that, for shooting was easy, an impersonal act, but thrusting the harpoon required skill and judgement, as it needed to be done accurately in order to preserve the seal fur, and also promptly, so as to shorten the seal's suffering. The Inuits believed in the environment; they believed that the seal, being Man's ancestor, gave its life so that Man could live, and hence Man, in return, had to show compassion and kill them by inflicting minimal suffering.

It has been said that the Inuits love seal liver and other entrails fresh, and would cut these out for immediate raw consumption. Benti was more concerned with getting the job done and then rushing home to do some house repairs during the short weekend.

Using the large hooked stick, he dragged the seal into the water and onto the boat, while leaving the head sticking out over the water.

As our boat sped away, blood continued to spurt from the seal, leaving a trail of blood in what was otherwise clear, crystal blue waters of the Greenland Sea.

"The fur would make a good coat," Benti said. The seal was young and would taste nice in soup. Older seals were normally left for the dogs. The bones would go to the village artisans, while the skin would go to the government tannery. Times were bad. Animal rights campaigners in the West had destroyed the seal skin market and prices had collapsed. The Greenland Home Rule Government, through the Royal Greenland Company, had just reduced the price of seals by half, to only DKK250. In reality, it was worth only DKK80, the price at which the government would sell the skins to the few tanneries that had survived the world boycott against animal skins. In other words, the government effectively subsidised these subsistence hunters. Benti said, "My father is a great seal hunter, respected by everyone on the island, and my mother used to spend all her time scaling and cleaning sealskins." Now, with the low prices, they were better off just using the skins for household purposes and collecting unemployment benefit from the Danish welfare state.

Mind you, this was not some big game hunter whom many would have considered to be despicable. He was an average Eastern Greenlander, 80% of whom were engaged in subsistence hunting — hunting for survival, like their ancestors had done so for thousands of years.

Benti thrust the harpoon through the seal's eyes, killing the creature instantly to minimise its suffering. This is the reality of life in the harsh wilderness of Greenland, where seals are not endangered and are precious traditional sources of meat.

They hunted for enough food to feed themselves and their dogs and did not believe in taking more than they needed. Indeed, Benti was an environmentalist of sorts. He placed the crisp wrappers and other pieces of rubbish in a corner of the boat, instead of throwing them overboard as people elsewhere would have done.

For the Eastern Greenlandic Inuit who live in this harsh land (85% covered by permanent ice) where no agriculture or animal farming is possible, the hunting of seals, which are not endangered species, is one of their very few means of subsistence survival. There are more than 5 million seals in Greenland, with 70,000 taken every year. Seal is a primary source of meat for the Inuits and the fur, a by-product. The selling of the skin to the Government provides some dignity and spare cash for a people who would otherwise have had to sit at home receiving unemployment benefits to send their children to school, for repairs to their houses (no, they do not stay in igloos) and thick clothing for winter.

Seal skin export used to be the largest source of export income for Greenland, but this had collapsed since a US ban was imposed in 1972. Unemployment was prevalent and I saw many people sitting around without anything to do. This has left the Inuit people susceptible to alcoholism, domestic violence and suicide. Alcohol consumption per capita was double that of Denmark, and suicide and homicide accounted for an amazing 11% and 3% of all deaths, respectively.

Suddenly, Benti raised his rifle again. His razor sharp eyes had spotted another seal, this time in the water. The seal popped its head out of the water, then swam towards us. "Young one," said Benti; they were inexperienced and not fearful of mankind.

"Come to your death," he said. Although this would have sounded distasteful to others, the Inuit were actually a straightforward people who had little time for flowery language. Outsiders, they said, spoke too much, and shook the fragile world with bombastic words.

Bang! A few bubbles, then the seal sank underneath the surface of the water.

"Shit," Benti muttered. We sped to the spot. There was some blood on the surface, but the seal had sunk below. "Gone to the sharks," he said. "If you don't get to the seal fast, they may sink and you would have wasted your bullets."

As we navigated in the fjord, Benti suddenly shouted, "Look there! Polar bear!" A gigantic silhouette of a bear was on an ice slab some distance away, looking as though it was scanning the water for live dinner. Benti seemed to freeze for a few moments, and then relaxed, saying, "It's OK, just a natural ice sculpture that looks like a polar bear." We might have been predators on the hunt for seals, but things were never clear-cut with polar bears, a well-known man-eater. One's instincts with polar bears might well be to escape from it, although an Inuit may sometimes decide to take the risk and attempt to shoot it for the bear's beautiful fur and save the meat for special festivals and events.

We continued the search for more seals. It was exciting and I was not bothered with the cold winds. Then we saw another moving object on a floating ice slab ahead. Benti turned to me and said, "This is your chance to shoot a seal."

There was no time for wishy-washy urbanite thoughts. Seals may look cute, but such an image was created by cartoonists. I was amongst hunters who had consumed it as a staple diet for thousands of years and I was being offered the honour of participating in their ancient ritual.

I took over the rifle — not having touched one since my army days — and fit it into my shoulder cave. The ease of movement betrayed some distant familiarity and it was a feeling that came with a bit of nostalgia. The seal was turning itself on the icepack. I took aim, held my breath and pressed the trigger slowly. Bang! I jerked a little. There was a smell of gunpowder in the air. The seal was hit and the ice around it was slowly turning red with its blood. It was a magnificent Greenlandic seal in a white coat with black spots. "A beautiful one," Benti said, as he thrust the harpoon into its eye and swiftly ended its misery.

The seal was too heavy for us to carry onto the boat. We dragged it across a water puddle to the other side of the huge ice slab, staining it red in the process. "Be careful," shouted Benti, "the ice may be thin!" A step onto thin ice would have meant certain death, or if one was lucky, a bad douse in the icy water, which was cold enough to be used by the Inuits as a natural refrigerator for their raw meat. We tied ropes on the ends of the enormous creature and then slowly dragged it back to the boat. We laid it across the front of the boat, causing it to tilt slightly to the front. We had to rearrange the first seal and the other contents of the boat so as to maintain a steady equilibrium in the water.

And so we went on, hunting a total of seven seals, including two that I shot. By now, Benti's friends had radioed him with the football results: 5–1; Tasiilaq had won. "Nothing to cry over," Benti said. "Believe me, we people of Kulusuk would celebrate anyway, in spite of the loss."

It was getting dark when we decided to sail back to the village. A

Greenland: Ice, ice everywhere in this land named Green. Perhaps the greatest real estate misnomer in world history?

lot more ice had drifted into the sound and we faced real difficulty in navigating our course. Benti was not deterred, ramming ice slabs which he deemed to be slow drifters. I was naturally worried, for it looked as though he might have sunk the boat at any moment. I should not have worried, for Benti was an experienced boatman. He slowed down when he felt the ice was drifting too fast and rammed at the slower ones to open up a path for us.

The temperature was dropping rapidly and I was getting sleepy, having slept only a few hours the night before. I huddled down against my backpack and the safety jackets to reduce the exposure of my body to the howling wind. I knew I could not afford to fall asleep as it was too dangerous in such extremely cold weather, remembering how I nearly froze to death in the mountains of Morocco. I thought of singing to keep myself awake, but decided against it and hummed a few nursery rhymes instead, as I battled desperately against the cold. The lights of Kulusuk soon came into sight. We passed the bright disco lights of the Community Hall. Benti was right, Kulusuk's citizens were celebrating in spite of the loss. With that, I looked forward to yet another exciting day in Greenland.

Immaqa (Maybe), I Will Be Out Tomorrow

Although it takes only two hours to fly from Iceland to Greenland, there is a world of difference between the two places. The Gulf Stream has bestowed upon Iceland much greenery but Greenland, in particular Kulusuk along the east coast just south of the Arctic Circle, is way off from the warm Gulf Stream. Granite rock, massive icebergs, bare haunting landscape with tiny pockets of greenery comprising mainly of grass and algae, and looming inland is the Greenland Icecap, which covers more than 85% of the world's largest island.

The Inuits were the first people of this island. In the 980s, Eric the Red — a Norwegian Viking who had repeatedly gotten into trouble in Norway and then Iceland — fled here, where he founded a colony. He then committed one of the greatest frauds in real estate industry history by naming the island 'Greenland' in order to attract settlers, in spite of the desolate coldness and hostile environment. The colony grew and then died suddenly in the 1400s, the cause of which still remains a mystery to historians. In 1721, the Danish re-established European settlement on the west coast of Greenland, mainly as a trading colony. They ruled for the next 200 years or so, until 1979, when Greenland was declared an autonomous nation within the Kingdom of Denmark, named Kalaallit Nunaat (meaning 'Land of the People'), with its own national flag and Prime Minister.

Over 20 years later, the Greenlandic or East Inuit language has become the island's first language and Danish the second. Greenlanders above 40 years old tend to speak Danish better. The civil service is largely Greenlandic as well and there are more Inuit signs than Danish ones. However, like most small remote nations, economic independence is an illusion. Most of the national budget is funded by Denmark. Everything in the supermarket is Danish. Job prospects remain poor and most services, from air transport to seal hunting, are subsidised by the Greenland Home Rule Government which, in turn, is funded by the Danish taxpayer.

***

Greenlandic Inuit children in traditional dress.

Kulusuk, where I had flown into, is the air hub of what is known as Tunu, or the 'Backside' of Greenland, which covers the eastern half of the country. Of the country's 56,000 people, only 4,000 live in this region, which is equivalent to half the size of Western Europe. This region is extremely isolated, blocked by ice for nine months out of twelve, with provisions supplied by only three icebreakers from July to September. If one were to visit in May, most of the grocery stores would be empty.

The skin of a polar bear adorns the wall of the airport terminal (which is nothing more than three average-sized rooms). It was one of two shot on the airport runway in 1994. Polar bears are dangerous creatures. They are feared as well as loved. They are man-eaters, the most powerful creatures of the realm, but they are also perceived as the embodiment of the human spirit in this harsh land. Indeed, they appear everywhere, from ancient legends to corporate logos and Greenland's national coat of arms.

***

I walked into the village, which was about 4km from the airport. Snowcapped mountains surrounded us and the numerous icebergs reflected the glaring sunlight from the sea. Eagles hovered around in the sky, while occasional gunshots sounded from hunters shooting

The cemetery at Kulusuk, East Greenland. This is a harsh land of permafrost and surreal beauty.

seals and whales from afar. The overall beauty and serenity was deceptive. Summer temperatures range between 0°C and 15°C, but sudden temperature drops could happen anytime. The water in the village harbour was a good reflection of the low temperatures: the locals had corpses of seals sunk into the harbour as the cold water acted as a natural refrigerator. In addition, although polar bear sightings were rare in summer, their presence was always a possibility.

Years ago, a woman was killed in a polar bear attack. The locals believed that it was either the work of *tupilak*, spirits out for vengeance on the command of evil-doers, or the woman had asked the *tupilak* to commit crimes but the *tupilak* had turned on her instead when it encountered a stronger *tupilak* guarding her enemies. Well, this region had only been converted to Christianity in the 1920s. The old gods remained powerful.

This is also the land of semi-permafrost. Tombs are shallow and the dead are often stored for months before burial in warmer months, when the soil can be dug. Indeed, there was no sewerage system — toilets were nothing more than large buckets to be emptied from time to time — and few houses had running water and electricity; the ground is too hard for modern conveniences like these.

***

Earlier, I had gotten in touch with Michael and Mette Nielsen, a Danish couple who had moved here with their three children two years ago. They had decided that they had had enough of nine-to-five jobs in Denmark and wanted a more fulfilling family life in a faraway land. In this isolated land, their children have grown up faster than those living in less remote locations. I was amazed at the maturity and intelligence of their eldest son, Rasmus, who at 11 years old spoke good English, Danish and Inuit, and was well versed in general knowledge, including bicycle repair, computers and just about every practicality required of one living in such a remote place.

The Nielsens ran a travel service of sorts, rented out one of their houses and helped to arrange hikes and excursions. I was given this most enlightening instruction: walk 4.5km from the airport, past the hotel and the cemetery, and look out for the first blue house on the left when you enter the village. As vague as it sounded, I somehow managed to find their house and was warmly received. The first day was spent on an unexpected seal hunt, a wonderful experience, and I went to bed amidst the symphonic howling and wailing of the village huskies. As every family kept at least a pack of 15 or more huskies for winter transportation, there were definitely more dogs than humans in this village.

***

I woke up early on Sunday, which was not surprising as the sun rose about as early as 2am. Rasmus walked me around the island's wild mountains and icy slopes and across fast-flowing rivers and bright green-yellow meadows with strange algae and scattered grass patches. It was amazing how Greenland had turned this boy into a man at so young an age. He seemed to know the island like the back of his hand. We brought along a husky, just in case we encountered a polar bear. The husky, a strong and brave creature, would not have hesitated to pounce on a polar bear ten times its size, giving us humans time to make our escape. We also explored ancient Inuit tombs, looking into the stony graves, mere piles of stones on top of skeletons — one could see the eyes of death in the skulls of hunters who had departed hundreds of years ago — which stared back at us with much sadness.

We spent the evening talking about life on the island, about how the Inuits lived, about serious problems like alcoholism and suicide, the results of unemployment and seasonal depression. The latter was a common syndrome in places where winter lasted more than half the year and there was a lack of light, causing severe depression. We spoke about the chronic homesickness of the Inuits, which meant very few were educated beyond primary school, because those who went beyond had to move to Nuuk, the capital, where they became homesick and often disrupted their studies to return home. Those who went further had to move to Denmark, where many succumbed to alcoholism and drugs in a failed accelerated transformation from small village life to modern urban civilisation.

***

On Monday, I went to the airport to catch a helicopter to Tasiilaq, the regional capital and largest town (with only 1,400 people) on the east coast of Greenland. The helicopter service was run by Alpha Air and was the only regular mode of transportation into and out of Tasiilaq. However, after waiting for half an hour, it was announced that the service could not run that day, as Eastern Greenland's sole air controller had fallen sick. With that, the capital of a region half the size of Western Europe was cut off from the outside world. That left the only other method of transportation by sea. I walked back to the village, where Mette arranged for an Inuit to sail me to Tasiilaq on his small boat, which was not the best mode of transport as it meant that I would have to brave the cold winds and icebergs once again, which I had had enough of on Saturday.

Anyway, I managed to reach Tasiilaq after an hour of icebergs and strong winds. There, I took two hours to see its mini-museum, supermarket (where I failed to find packed seal and whale meat — these were caught by locals for domestic consumption, not for sale), church, philatelic bureau (one of the largest local employers) and bookshop. There was not much to do and I wanted to have lunch at the local hotel. I was greeted with a "Sorry, we don't serve meals after 1pm." No, not even coffee. I asked the tourist office where I could sit down for a snack and tea. This was Greenland. No cafes were available (well, one was open, but I did not fancy having ice cream, al fresco, in the wind) and restaurants (only two in the whole of the east coast) did not serve beyond 1pm. In any case, the kind lady at the tourist office allowed me to stay in the tourist office to read my book and write my journal.

At 5pm, I returned to Kulusuk on the boat and had a nice dinner of seal meat with the Nielsens. The seal meat, given by Benti (who had brought me on the seal hunt), was done the Inuit way, simply boiled and salted. It tasted like beef, with grease and a fishy taste. Of course, the Nielsens had not introduced me to yet another Inuit favourite, fermented seal skin with local algae, which required more than three months' preparation and was not exactly endearing to the uninitiated.

***

I was to fly to Iceland the next day. The Inuits have a word, *Immaqa*, which means 'maybe', similar in meaning to the Arabic *Inshallah*. *Immaqa*, it will snow tomorrow. *Immaqa*, the icebergs may prevent us from sailing. *Immaqa*, there may be no seals tomorrow. *Immaqa*, if the air controller of the whole of East Greenland is not sick tomorrow, I could fly out of the country. Otherwise, I would be stuck here. Despite the wonderful landscape and friendly people, I needed less of the strong winds and icy temperature. *Immaqa*.

The Hallgrimskirkja Church in Reykjavik, Iceland, and its phallus-shaped steeple.

Huge Penises, Puffin Party and Rotten Shark

Size matters. It was a magnificent thing: uncut, a little wrinkled from age and frequency of use, but still impressive and fully erect at almost all times. It must have been most fertile and powerful in its heyday, and a conqueror of many birds, so to speak. Well, at 6ft, the penis of the sperm whale was taller than me and greeted visitors to the Icelandic Phallological Museum in Reykjavik, also the premises of the Icelandic Phallological Institute, i.e. Penis Museum, perhaps the only one of its kind in the world.

Here one sees the penises of the whale, dolphin, giraffe, bull, etc. — all much larger and longer than that of the human. Only one creature was missing here, that of the homo sapien, but the museum was proud to announce that a kind Icelander, currently in his 70s, has kindly pledged to donate his to the museum upon his demise. So much for completeness.

***

I reached Reykjavik at 3pm local time on Tuesday. I almost did not manage to get onto the flight as someone had screwed up my booking and I had to be placed on the waiting list instead. Nonetheless, I should have considered myself lucky that the plane did fly after all. The sole air controller of East Greenland had recovered from his flu and the region's links with the outside world had been restored. I was the last to board the plane and had barely done so when it took off. I saw the last of Greenland, those magnificent snow-covered mountains, endless glaciers and countless floating icebergs — the latter like stars in the sky, except that they were in the sea.

Upon arrival, I rushed to see the giant penises, passing by the phallus-shaped steeple of the Hallgrimskirkja Church (everything in Reykjavik had started to look like penises) and walked around the nice old town. It was pleasant and easy. The weather was gorgeous, after the stirring cold of Greenland. Reykjavik was founded in 874AD by Ingolfur Arnarson, yet another Norwegian Viking outlawed in his homeland and forced to flee westward. Arnarson saw land and threw his pillars overboard, whereupon they floated ashore and Arnarson decided that this was his destiny. Here he founded Reykjavik, or Smoky Bay.

Here was a nice city where everybody seemed to speak better English than some of the folks in East London, York and Glasgow. The people were also liberal and freedom-loving — they were the first to recognise Lithuanian independence, well before the anti-Gorbachev coup occurred; and posters, brochures (distributed by the tourist office) and rainbow flags proclaimed the Gay Pride parade over the upcoming weekend — this would have shocked more conservative folks from Taleban-ruled Afghanistan, Saudi Arabia and the Christian right in the Bible Belt of USA and, yes, Singapore.

***

I continued my gastronomical adventure by looking for puffin meat, supposedly an Icelandic delicacy (with apologies to my animal/bird lover friends). There was some initial difficulty in finding a restaurant that served puffin, but I eventually found one, an upmarket restaurant with French-style service and Icelandic cuisine (no contradictions here). I chose the most exotic item in the menu, something quaintly named 'Puffin Party'. The three-course meal was priced at US$40, excluding wine, and comprised fresh salad with marinated puffin carpaccio and smoked and cured puffin with orange vinaigrette; puffin with honey-glazed vegetables and creamed Roquefort cheese sauce; and Granny's home-baked skyr cake with blueberry sorbet. The puffin tasted great. A kind of red meat with little fat. Tougher than chicken, but more tender than beef. Wonderful!

***

Iceland is a geography teacher's dream but a natural disaster rescue team's nightmare. A land that stands on the American-Eurasian fault-line, Iceland has just about everything a geography buff would be interested in, from old and new volcanoes, geysers and hot springs, to icebergs, glaciers and the Arctic Circle. The line crosses Icelandic territory at an island named Grimsey, which provides Air Iceland with the excuse to run day tours for tourists who want to cross the line and receive a certificate to frame on their wall. Contrary to my usual practice, I restrained myself from this particular touristy activity.

The underground heat, volcanoes, etc., not only provide the whole country with a cheap source of power (which also translates into many hot baths everywhere, which is great if one is used to the all-pervasive smell of sulphur), but also numerous tourist attractions where tour guides show off their knowledge on what happens when sudden lava flows cover a cold swampy ground (strange and cute volcano-like craters called pseudo-craters are formed) or when seawater algae mixes with silica mud in the lava (they become a pond of bluish-looking chemical waste water that the Icelanders market as the 'Blue Lagoon' to entice tourists who would otherwise not pay to swim in it).

Everywhere, tourists are led to see hot water emerging from nowhere (great if one needs a hot bath in the desert, but please take note of the temperature) and boiling mud where the mad cook eggs or make bread (why do they not do it at home?). Of course, the downside

Forces of nature: Iceland has some of Europe's greatest waterfalls.

of sitting between the Americas and Europe are lots of earthquakes, volcanic eruptions, sudden glacial floods and Americans who make short stopover breaks en route to Europe.

***

I spent three days wandering around the Northeast of Iceland, visiting numerous strange geological formations resulting from various permutations of volcanic lava combining with floods, cold water, hot water, soft rock, hard rock, ice and snow. There were spectacular landscapes, including lakes, rivers, black desert and Europe's largest and tallest waterfalls. This was indeed a land of sheer natural beauty, one that was pristine and almost empty. After all, there were only 280,000 people living in an area of 103,000 sq km.

***

I decided to try my luck with whale watching in the tiny town of Husavik in northern Iceland. Hopping onto an oak boat, I found myself in a rocking, floating bowl on the rough waters of the Arctic Ocean. Here, free from the safe shelter of icebergs present in the waters off Greenland, the boat swayed like a cradle shaken by a lunatic. I found my stomach rising to my throat and rushed quickly to the bow, where the entrance to the toilet was located.

Unfortunately, the inevitable happened: my inner volcano erupted like Mt Etna and the gory contents of my breakfast — including those wonderful salmon slices on Icelandic bread — landed across the deck like lava on the plains. It took me a few moments to regain my composure, clean myself and apologise sheepishly to the crew. The rest of the whale watch was most uneventful. No humpbacks, no water-spurting whales. Just a few exposed fins above the water. I had seen more of a whale on the seal hunt in Greenland, but that incident of whale spotting was unplanned and unintended, and as a result, no photographs were taken.

I deserted the boat in a rush upon its return to harbour, and managed to catch the next bus to Akureyri, where I secured a flight to Reykjavik, well ahead of my original schedule. I had decided that I had had enough of wild landscapes and wanted a bit of wining and dining, as well as pseudo-metropolitan nightlife (pseudo-metropolitan because that was as much as one could get in a capital city with only 170,000 people). Well, perhaps that was not a fair comment, as Reykjavik was indeed well equipped for a great night out, despite its size. Possibly on a per capita basis, this city had more international restaurants, bars and clubs than most cities in the world.

***

Being the gastronomical adventurer that I was, I made another foray into the brave new world of exotic dishes. This time, I asked for *hakarl*, shark meat buried in sand for six months to a year to ensure sufficient decomposition — it was supposed to smell like stool — a traditional Icelandic delicacy that mad foreigners like myself love to try. Indeed, the waitress said that it seemed the foreigners loved *hakarl* better than they did. I was served a small quarter-matchbox cube of it. I could not seem to smell what I was supposed to be expecting, either because my nose had become insensitive after the whale watch or the restaurant had tried its best to moderate the smell for foreigners. Actually, there was a faint smell, but it was nothing compared to that famous Southeast Asian 'king of fruits', the durian.

After dinner, I set off to explore the nightlife of Reykjavik, but discovered an empty town with no one but foreigners hanging around waiting for something to happen. Eating and drinking in Reykjavik was expensive and most Icelanders stayed home to have their dinner before coming out late at night. Suddenly, close to midnight, Reykjavik came alive again, with youngsters wandering around and traffic congestion in the city centre. The city of the midnight sun was also the city of midnight traffic jams!

I hung around a few bars and danced until the wee hours with some Vietnamese-Icelandic girls in a downtown club — the legacy of the boat people who arrived in the 1970s/1980s. I emerged from a club in the early hours to a Reykjavik full of drunken teenagers and more traffic congestion.

The next two days were spent visiting more geysers, waterfalls and craters, plus a dip into the chemical waste known as the Blue Lagoon. I hopped by a museum, had another wild night in a club, and then made a last attempt to find puffin meat in a fish market. Well, I did find the puffin meat, but wisely decided that I would probably have spoilt the meat by attempting to cook it. It was best to keep good memories where they were supposed to be.

Afterthoughts: Small Countries Rich and Poor

The natural environment and landscape of Greenland and Iceland were dramatic, but I tend to be captivated by places with a stronger sense of ethnic diversity or exotic cultures and Iceland clearly did not have that. Greenland was just too windy and cold for a son of the tropics to fully appreciate and enjoy. I felt worn out everyday from the cold, although some of my experiences there, such as the seal hunt, were just extraordinary. It was something I would remember for a long time.

There were many aspects of this trip that were thought provoking: seal hunting, the economics of living in a harsh land like Greenland, and the economics of running a small nation like Iceland.

Seal Hunting

Strangely enough, an email I had sent on the seal hunt provoked a number of responses from my normally quiet readership. Most of those who responded thought that it was an interesting experience, but there were also a few who felt that seal hunting was cruel and should be banned. One interesting point to note was the fact that many people used terms such as 'seal clubbing' or 'mass cruelty', even though:

- there was no mass clubbing of seals involved or described in the email (it was amazing how these individuals were able to perceive things that did not happen);
- there was no mass killing because the hunter (usually alone) has to search for small numbers of individual seals in a very small boat (a mere 2 metres in length) through dangerous icebergs in hostile weather conditions; and
- the use of the harpoon may have sounded cruel, but it was the most humane way of killing a seal after it had been injured by a bullet as it finished the animal before it suffered excessively from the wound.

It is easy for individuals sitting in their comfortable armchairs to cry out for animal rights, but to the Eastern Greenlandic Inuit who live in a harsh land (85% covered by permanent ice) with no agriculture and animal farming possible, the hunting of seals, which are not endangered, is one of their very few means of subsistence survival.

As mentioned earlier, Greenland is plagued with many social issues such as unemployment and alcoholism. On a macro level, these point to another interesting question: can a harsh environment like Greenland support a viable economy?

Greenland

This is a country (or rather, an autonomous state within the Kingdom of Denmark) with 56,000 people who are spread across an island the size of the European Union. Most of the country is covered with permanent ice and apart from 14,000 people living in Nuuk (previously known as Godthab), the capital, the rest of the population lives in over 60 towns and villages scattered along the small strip of land along the coast which is not covered by ice. Only 4,000 people live in the remote eastern half of the island that is cut off by ice for 9 months a year.

Seal skin products, primarily by-products of Inuit subsistence hunting, used to be the largest source of export income but that has long since collapsed (together with tanneries and skin processing factories). Sixty per cent of Greenland's GDP comprises direct subsidies from Denmark (US$410m) and the largest source of export earnings is from fish and seafood products (85%). The latter is comprised mainly of licensing fees earned from foreign fishing fleets, although the Royal Greenland Company, Greenland's largest company, also owned by the Greenland Home Rule Government, makes some of these earnings. There is some mining (which is actively encouraged by the government), but such activities are hardly significant.

On top of that, 20% of the population are not born in Greenland, they are mostly Danish people who work in branches of the civil service, education and various technical or professional positions. As such, a relatively small portion of the GDP relates to economic activity that involves the indigenous Greenlander. About two-thirds of these work in the civil service. If one is cynical, one could say that

Quaint houses in the village of Kulusuk, Greenland. It isn`t just Danish architecture that has been transplanted into the Arctic, but also the Danish welfare state, with a whole host of unintended consequences.

the bulk of the employed Greenlanders work to distribute Danish subsidies to the population. This is hardly surprising, as this is a land which is hardly conducive to any form of economic activity or human habitation.

Agriculture and animal farming is hardly possible given the climate and natural environment. Industrialisation is not feasible due to the small population (imagine putting out an advertisement for 2,000 electronics factory positions in a country where the capital has only 14,000 people) and high transportation costs arising from the weather and the remoteness of location. ("... the port is frozen today and will be for the next six months, can we ship the semi-conductor chip in summer time?")

Mining has been actively encouraged, but quantities found so far have been either small or simply uneconomical considering extraction costs (try digging for gold in permafrost when the locals are not even able to bury their dead in winter) and remoteness of location. Even retailing can be difficult here: how does one supply goods to 56,000 people who are spread across a country the size of Western Europe? The cost of doing so would be extraordinarily high. Indeed, there is only one supermarket chain and it is state-owned. For the goods to be affordable (at prices slightly higher than in Europe), even those in the existing solitary chain are subsidised.

Before the Danish people arrived, the Inuits lived by just hunting for seals, polar bears and whales. They probably died young from disease and lack of nutrition. Now, they live to 68 years of age with the benefit of modern healthcare and the acquisition of a more varied diet which includes imported vegetables, pork, beef, lamb, cheese, bread and all the things that we would find in a supermarket. All of these have to be imported as little can be produced in this fragile environment with scarce natural resources.

The hunting of seals and granting of fishing licenses, even in the best of years, can hardly support an economy that has to pay for all these modern amenities and new necessities. As such, the Danish welfare state steps in to provide the necessary cash. That is why many are unemployed and live by collecting unemployment benefits, and hence suffer from the accompanying loss of morale and depression. As mentioned earlier, alcoholism has become a common problem and people die from suicide and alcohol-related diseases.

There is no easy solution. Tourism may bring additional income, and this has been increasing over the years. However, the number of tourists remains small. The lack of flights and high costs remain obstacles to tourism development. The former is a chicken and egg situation — if there are few flights, tickets are expensive and tourists are deterred from coming; if there are few tourists, few airlines have the incentive to fly there. Perhaps Greenland could learn from Iceland (which has succeeded in diverting America-to-Europe air traffic to stop over in Iceland, which in turn sparked off the Icelandic tourism industry), but that may have been an exceptional case and difficult to emulate.

A potential bright spot may well be America's new Star Wars plan, which may result in the redeployment of old US outer defense radar, air and missile bases in Greenland. This could provide employment and even infrastructure development.

I suspect all these point to one conclusion, that given the harsh environment, Greenland simply cannot support its current population size. If Denmark decides to abandon Greenland and stop all subsidies one day, most of the population, who in any case have Danish citizenship, could emigrate to Denmark. It would be a sad outcome, this destruction of an ancient lifestyle, which, in any case, has been supported by artificial non-market forces for many years.

Iceland

Whilst Greenland is obviously a poor country heavily dependent on handouts, Iceland, on the other hand, is one of the richest countries in the world. It has a modern, developed economy with one of the highest standards of living anywhere. It has a small population (280,000) living on an island of 103,000km², the size of a medium-sized country. It may be on the same latitude as Greenland, but Iceland certainly does not deserve its icy name. As they say, 'Greenland is ice and Iceland is green'.

Last week, I stood by the Arctic Ocean near Husavik, northeast Iceland, just south of the Arctic Circle. Here, farmers were packing their hay while lambs wandered around. A few hundred kilometres to the west in Greenland, also just south of the Arctic Circle, people do nothing but hunt, as the cold kills off all farm creatures and no agriculture is possible. Iceland has benefited from the warm Gulf Stream, not only in terms of agriculture but also from the rich sea life it brings to Iceland. This has made Iceland the 11th most important fishing nation. Given their productivity and efficiency in harvesting this natural resource, Iceland has been able to achieve its current standard of living.

The fishing industry has also provided a high standard of education and the development of R & D-based life sciences and IT industries, all of which help to further diversify the country's sources of income. Iceland also lies in a geothermal sensitive region, and income from fishing has been invested in sophisticated equipment to tap this important source of energy. Most of Iceland's heating and electricity is generated domestically from its geothermal resources. This has resulted in

One of the many thermal power generating plants found across Iceland.

enormous savings for the country. There are many poor countries in the world that lie on geothermal belts, e.g. Indonesia, Philippines, Kamchatka Peninsula in Russia, but few have the prerequisites to harvest such resources.

Having said that, Iceland has not always been a rich country. Before World War II, this was a poor country where famine was a frequent occurrence (killing a large percentage of the population), not to mention other natural disasters such as volcano eruptions and earthquakes. Incidents of whales getting stuck in the shallows, now considered undesirable, used to be greeted by Icelanders as the equivalent of winning the lottery, as they helped to alleviate hunger and saved the local population from starvation. In the past, Icelanders emigrated to look for new land and for survival; these days, emigration arises because of boredom.

The turning point for Iceland came during World War II, when the British occupied Iceland in 1940 after Denmark, Iceland's colonial master, had been invaded by the Germans. The British brought

employment to this poor country and began a huge infrastructure construction programme. Airports and roads were built throughout the country as part of the war effort against the Germans. They left in 1941 and were replaced by the Americans. The 65,000 American soldiers continued the British construction efforts and virtually transformed this country, which then had only a population of 120,000. There must have been as many American soldiers as there were Icelandic men!

The whole economy was injected with cash and blessed with new infrastructure, which allowed the country to develop further after the war. Not many countries have succeeded in transforming themselves so radically after foreign occupation! Iceland was, by that time, a country with a long tradition of education — compulsory universal education was introduced in the mid-19th century when self-government was declared. The Icelandic church also plays an active part in preserving the Icelandic language through mass education, which meant that Icelanders could easily launch their national development by riding on the British and American occupations.

The Icelandic experience is unique and not easily replicable elsewhere. What is also remarkable is their ability to preserve their language, spoken by only 280,000 people. With such a small population, publishing a book or a newspaper, much less operating television channels in the Icelandic language, must be very costly. Indeed, how does one manage a whole country with its own spoken language with a population of only 280,000 people?

Nonetheless, the Icelanders publish the largest number of books in the world on a per capita basis, mostly translations of foreign publications into the Icelandic language, and they have even produced a Nobel Prize winner in literature. The costs of these must be tremendous but probably well subsidised by the Icelandic economy. Things are, therefore, expensive in Iceland, but their economy is able to support it, and the Icelandic people see the preservation of their language as a matter of national pride.

As a side note, Icelanders are obsessed with sagas: long stories of heroes, gods and their deeds. They are often long and complicated, full of sub-plots and multiple twists and turns, as well as moral messages, some of which can be confusing. Despite a similar Viking heritage, no other Scandinavian country has the equivalent of an Icelandic saga.

Every Icelander grows up familiar with these sagas. It is said that a student once requested a taxi driver to fetch him home for free, as he had no money. The taxi driver agreed, provided the student could answer a difficult riddle from one of the more obscure sagas. The student agreed and was actually able to provide the right answers, thus earning himself a regular free taxi trip. What is remarkable about this story is that there are very few taxi drivers in the world who know scholarly sagas well enough to derive a difficult riddle, and it is equally surprising that the student would have been able to answer such a riddle correctly. Well, Iceland has done all the right things in the past, and was able to ride on the developments of World War II (which was beyond its control), and it has succeeded in transforming itself thoroughly. This is the real saga of modern Iceland.

POSTSCRIPT:

The advent of global warming has led to significant changes to Greenland — in fact, Greenland will be one of the few countries in the world to benefit from global warming. Whilst the rapid retreat and thinning of the Greenlandic glaciers is likely to contribute to the rise in sea levels, it will also potentially allow mining and oil extraction activities to take place in what was previously a terrain prohibitively expensive to exploit. In fact, the melting of the glaciers has already led to a great deal of experimentation in agriculture in southern Greenland and a boom in tourism in areas where permafrost had previously made travel difficult and costly. With financial independence becoming a feasible prospect, nationalists in Greenland are aggressively charting the route towards eventual complete independence from Denmark. Greenland has recently passed a referendum that grants the country greater self-government.

Iceland, on the other hand, became a victim of its success in 2008. Iceland's ability to attract short-term lending in the past few decades had allowed the country to build a financial empire of banks and industrial companies across Europe; but its inability to renew such lending as a result of the global financial crisis led instead to the collapse of its three largest banks and the near collapse of its economy. It remains to be seen if the former miracle land of the North Sea can rise again.

Faroe Islands — Green Mountainous Heaven (2002)

Green layered mountains rising steeply from the ocean, little streams of blue plunging off cliffs and forming rainbow falls, matchbox houses of black and red crowned with lush green turf rooftops, round-horn sheep frolicking with seabirds on minute corners of greenery scattered over walls of battered rock cliffs. Legend has it that God's foremen clipped His fingernails at Creation and the 18 fragments of nails which fell into the sea formed the Faroe Islands.

The Faroe Islands, the Islands of Sheep, were once known as such to the ancient Viking mariners. Located between Scotland and Iceland on the far reaches of the North Atlantic, it is often joked that the Faroe Islands were settled by Vikings who became seasick while sailing to Iceland. This mountain land provides little arable land, but the warm Gulf Stream provides plenty of fish and lush green pastures for sheep despite the latitude. The islands were a free Viking republic at first (with their Constitution, the *Seyoabraevio*, the 'Sheep Letter') but later fell under Norwegian and then Danish rule. Since 1948, the islands have been self-governing, with their own Prime Minister, flag, banknotes (Faroese Kroner, which is on 1:1 parity with the Danish Kroner) and stamps.

***

I arrived at the Faroe Islands on a flight from Aberdeen, Scotland. Apart from a few tourists, the Atlantic Airways (the national airline) flight also carried quite a few British oilmen. The Faroe Islands struck oil two years ago and oilmen were still trying to verify the commercial viability of oil extraction.

The hottest political issue then was independence. A proud nation strongly aware of its distinctive culture and language (similar to Icelandic and Old Norse), the Faroe Islands always had an independence movement. In fact, when I passed the sole Danish military camp on a tour bus, the Faroese driver jokingly called it the 'Camp of the Occupation Army', much to the discomfort of the solitary Danish tourist on board, who did not find it funny. However, the Faroes Home Rule Government, which receives an annual DKK1 billion (US$120m) subsidy, has a track record of asking the Danish state to bail it out (twice in the past 30 years), which did not inspire support for independence in this tiny nation of 48,000 people, that is, until the discovery of oil. Suddenly, dreams of a North Atlantic Kuwait emerged and in the last elections, support for pro-independence parties rose to 50% of the electorate. Any confirmation of the commercial viability of the oil would surely push the support beyond current levels.

Flying to the Faroe Islands was a little adventure of sorts. Planes often arrived to find it impossible to land due to excessive fog on the

Traditional doorway in an old Faroe house.

short runways of Vagar Airport. I have met people whose two-hour flight from Copenhagen had to be turned back due to fog. Thank goodness I was lucky.

A clear blue sky and wondrous cliff views greeted me as I landed at Vagar Airport. It was summer time in the North Atlantic and this meant almost 24 hours of sunlight. Within hours of arriving, I was sipping coffee in a café and admiring the sunset at 11:30pm. It never really got dark and streetlights were never switched on. At 2am, it was as bright as a mid-afternoon Barcelona summer day, although the temperature betrayed the latitude of the land.

***

Torshavn, the capital of the Faroe Islands, is a quaint little town of 16,000 inhabitants. It markets itself as 'the smallest capital city in the world'. They seem to have forgotten that short of full independence, they have to compete for that title with other entities like Turks & Caicos, Cayman Islands and other sundry isles, mostly remnants of the old British empire. In any case, it is a small town with a nice country feel and really friendly and laidback people. It still lives in an age where doors are unlocked and one's hotel landlord is too shy to ask for payment in advance. That was probably what the world used to be like a hundred years ago. One wonders if the discovery of oil will change that eventually.

***

The Faroe Islands are beautiful. I spent the next few days exploring the dramatic seaside mountain views and the many picturesque fishing villages that lined the shores. With generous Danish subsidies, the Faroes have built a good system of highways complete with bridges (including one known as the 'Bridge Across the Atlantic' because it links two islands), tunnels and mountain hugging roads.

A new undersea tunnel had just been built linking Vagar (where the airport is located) and Stremoy, where Torshavn is located. All this for 48,000 inhabitants. It all sounded similar to the notorious Japanese programme of building roads, tunnels and bridges to remote islands, which was in reality a desperate attempt to utilise government spending to stimulate the economy.

***

The Faroe Islands are also famous for the *grindadrap*, the ancient Faroese method of driving whole schools of pilot whales into shallow bays, inserting steel gaffes into their blowpipes and then massacring them with long knives and machetes. This ancient custom is condemned by many environmentalists as cruel, and by those who believe that whales are endangered. Many are also shocked by pictures of the *grindadrap*, which is accompanied by massive bloodshed staining entire bays of water deep red. However, the Faroese argue that pilot whales are not endangered (800,000 of them in the North Atlantic) and their method is the most humane way of killing such huge creatures. Besides, the Faroese have been eating pilot whales for a whole millennium, and this accounts for 15% of the meat the islanders

Dramatic mountain views in the remote Faroes.

consume. The *grindadrap* is also a communal activity rather than a commercial venture, one which involves entire communities and the meat harvested is shared by the local people. It is a part of old Faroese culture, an activity that is celebrated by numerous paintings and public art pieces that I saw on the islands.

***

I would not say that the Faroe Islands are a gastronomical heaven, although they do have some interesting dishes. They love seabirds, especially puffins and seagull-related birds like fulmar and guillemots. Unfortunately, the restaurants do not necessarily have them all the time. The islanders tend to have them at home. In fact, a tour guide told me that to sample these dishes, one needed to put in a bit of effort by dressing well, visiting a disco and getting to know a local girl. Then it would be more than just Faroese food that one would experience — it would be bed and breakfast.

POSTSCRIPT:

The islands have remained a sleepy land, but Burger King arrived here a few years ago, exciting the international media seeking trivia. The country, in the meantime, has been making a gradual recovery since the collapse of the fishing industry in the 1990s. In 2008, Faroes even made a US$52m loan to Iceland following the latter's banking crisis.

CENTRAL AND SOUTHERN EUROPE

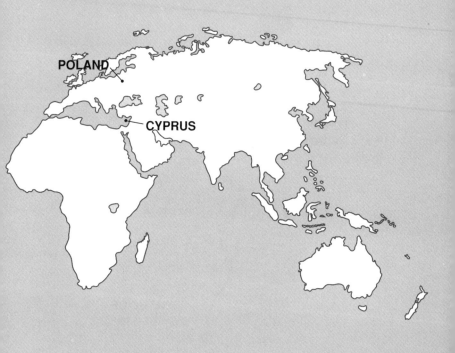

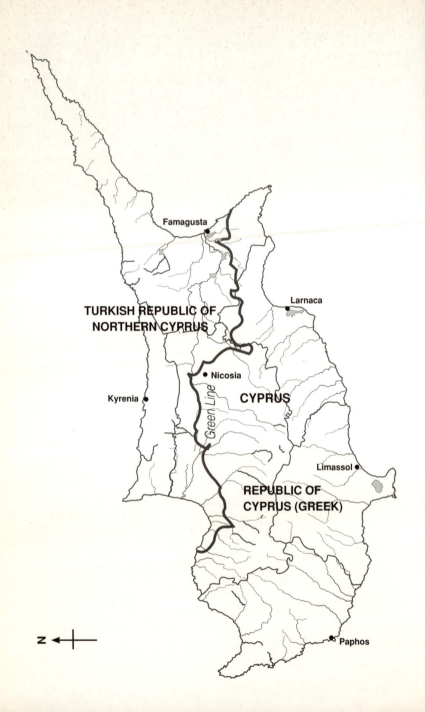

The Cypriot Trilogy
(2001)

Vulgar Scuffle with a Cypriot Gangster

"Chino, get back to work!" A bald stocky Cypriot patted my thigh as he waddled into the hotel lobby with a blonde, skinny lass in loud pink tights. What a rude bum he was, I thought, but I had no intention of getting distracted from my book while waiting for my friends to get ready for the second day of our Cypriot adventure.

The duo stood at the empty reception looking impatient, while the girl grumbled in her Russian accented English, "I had to go from one hotel to another... little hours... it's too much for me... I cannot go on like this too long..."

Caressing her hair gently, her companion comforted her, "Don't worry... we will sort that out... we will get this f___king hotel to..." His words, lost in thin air, betrayed a faint East London accent.

Obviously impatient with the wait, the idiotic bum turned around and shouted at me, "Hey Chino, where are your f___king bosses? Get them here immediately!"

What insolence!

I retorted, "I don't work here. I'm a tourist. I have no idea where the hotel people are."

The 'Natasha' (as Russian prostitutes were known) pulled his shirt, and the pimp turned around and gave her a polar bear kiss. She started her grumbling again...

I glanced at my watch. Twenty-five minutes had lapsed and my travel companions were nowhere in sight. Blame it on the seductive Cypriot wine we had last night.

The couple had enough of waiting and marched out of the hotel lobby. Scarcely a few steps from me, the Cypriot scumhead turned around and shouted at me, "Chino, tell your f__king bosses here that they should go screw themselves. F__k them, and f__k you, too!"

What had I done to deserve this? A peacenik like me doing nothing more than reading my *Lonely Planet* while waiting for my friends. First, he called me 'Chino', and then shouted at me with the infamous F-word. It was too much! I decided to press the nuclear button and return fire. So, I launched my seldom-used F-missile: "Hey, f__k you, too! I'm not working here and I'm not your f__king servant!"

The balding pig turned into a monster. He grabbed my shirt collar, pulled me close to his face — I could smell his fuming heat and his menacing eyes resembled the proverbial gates of Hell.

"What did you say? You scold me f__k!" He clenched his fist and gestured threateningly.

"F__k you! Say that again and I'll punch you. I'll kill you, f__king Chino!"

My mind raced across the Mediterranean and the plains of Eurasia. I saw the empty hill slopes of Bamiyan, Afghanistan, where the Taleban had recently destroyed the ancient Buddhas. Above the Ganges Plains I saw Lumbini, birthplace of Lord Buddha. Oh, how much bad karma had I accumulated by uttering the four-letter word, and in impatience with a less enlightened soul. I saw the tiny red dot that was Singapore and the silhouette of my family... In all of a split second, my decision was made. I kept quiet and smiled.

The man loosened his grip, turned around and walked out of the hotel.

Closing a 83,000,000 Lira Deal in a Rebel Capital

We closed a TL83,000,000 deal in a matter of minutes. We could not squeeze in any equity warrant or convertible option, but we got it settled in cash and that was all that mattered in such desolate frontiers. One would not want to spend too much for some complicated forex swap to hedge any extended exposure. Such deals could not be easier, especially in Lefkosa, the Turkish name for the northern half of Nicosia, capital of the unrecognised Turkish Republic of Northern Cyprus (TRNC), a political entity created as a result of the 1974 operations by Turkish forces.

Whilst the Greek-dominated Republic of Cyprus had recovered from the mayhem of the Turkish march which displaced half the Greek population and went on to prosper from tourism and financial services, the northern one-third of the island sank into an economic abyss with the lack of foreign investments and the burden of a pathetic Turkish economy. With the collapse of the Turkish lira the year before, we were paying TL83,000,000 or about US$75 for a full-day taxi tour of TRNC.

***

We arrived in the sunny Republic of Cyprus at 4am on a Saturday morning. We hopped into a rented car driven at 150km per hour, arriving in Nicosia in 20 minutes as opposed to the usual 45 minutes. We dumped our belongings in a mosquito-infested outfit called Tony's B & B (which *Lonely Planet* recommended — they were not right all the time; anyway, we moved to the cleaner, unlisted Rimi Hotel next door), then headed straight for the Green Line, the ceasefire line between the Greek and Turkish Cypriots policed by the United Nations.

As we neared the Green Line, flashy hotel facades and fast food kiosks suddenly gave way to run-down buildings with faded paints and sandbag bunkers; the only vestiges of brightness were the bright blue national colours of Greece. Young conscripts from Greece performed their National Service here in Cyprus, officially a separate country. Cypriot and Greek flags flapped above the bunkers. In fact, I probably saw more Greek flags than Cypriot ones. It appeared that the Republic of Cyprus made no secret of its Greek-orientation on the frontlines, while maintaining the image of being the only legitimate cross-racial body on international propaganda and diplomatic circuits. Indeed, as I was to discover, the Cypriot flag regained its prominence at the tourist-laden coastal resorts, as that was probably the image it preferred to show the world.

'UN Buffer Zone', 'Protected Area', 'No Photos, No Video' — the loud notices proclaimed as we hit the UN zone. Bored young faces in uniforms manned the watch towers in this touristy and most un-warlike of war zones. These handsome lads must have been dying for the day to be over in order to slip across to either (or both) sides of the Line to meet their girlfriends, mistresses and what-have-you. Frontiers were probably wonderful places for those who were two-timing their partners, as the other party would have found it difficult to discover his/her rival on the other side of the barb-wired line.

Walls on the Greek side were adorned with pictures of Turkish

Elderly ladies holding photos of their missing loved ones on the Greek Cypriot side of the Green Line.

atrocities (what about Greek atrocities?) and the traveller was greeted by elderly ladies in black mourning dress holding photos of their missing loved ones (victims of the barbaric Turkish invasion, as they called it) and handing out propaganda leaflets. Greek leaflets tended to highlight the struggle against British and Turkish Ottoman rule, while ignoring the breakdown of constitutional order in 1963, when the Greek-inspired change of Constitution deprived the Turks of their privileges, thus leading to communal fighting and the stationing of UN troops.

Nevertheless, I still found it hard to accept the uprooting of so many people in order to uphold the rights of a minority that comprised less than 20% of the nation's population. However, the Turkish Cypriot population could well have been faced with an ethnic cleansing of sorts in 1974 if extremist Greeks had their way and Turkey had not invaded Cyprus to save their ethnic brethren. This was such a small land: there were only slightly more than 600,000 Greeks versus 150,000 Turks, with the latter supported by 50 million Turks in Turkey.

The supposed genocide could have happened either way. This apparent calm aside, tension rose from time to time, coupled with occasional incidents, the last of which occurred in 1996, when a young Greek ran over to the Turkish side and pulled down the Turkish flag, only to be beaten to death. A few more deaths took place in the following days of clashes across the line. Cruel, but I doubt anyone would have allowed another person to desecrate his or her national flag.

The Greek Cypriots did not like people crossing to the other side and the rules were duly disseminated to the traveller via signboards — be back by 5pm, do not buy anything in the occupied zone, do not allow your passport to be stamped by the other side (i.e. no stamping by illegal states allowed). Tourist maps even highlighted the Turkish zone as 'Inaccessible due to illegal Turkish occupation' and the northern Ercan Airport was denounced as 'Certified unsafe' — what a sham, given that the Turkish Cypriots welcomed tourists with open arms and that scheduled and charter flights arrived from major international airports. All these reminded me of China's somewhat crude harassing of Taiwan in international circles.

The moment we entered the borders of TRNC, we were greeted with glossy posters of the sun, sea and more, Turkish edition. The immigration office was staffed with friendly unveiled girls, one of whom was dressed in such a tight shirt that it looked as though the twin bulky weights on her chest were about to burst through anytime. The stern stare of Turkey's founding father, Ataturk, shone from the walls, reminding one that this was a secular state where religion was something to tuck away at home rather than to proclaim and glorify.

With our TRNC entry pass on hand, we negotiated the TL83,000,000 deal and proceeded to explore TRNC in a taxi. While my travel companions dozed off from the overnight flight, I had a lively conversation with Mehmet, the driver.

Mehmet proclaimed himself a Turkish Cypriot (as opposed to Anatolian Turkish — the mainland Turks have flooded the island since the arrival of the Turkish army), and more Cypriot than Turkish. "We eat the same food and know each other's languages", he asserted. "We are one nation and yet not quite one."

Beneath this proclamation of togetherness, however, was pride in a separate identity and the desire to defend that identity through armed

Huge flag of the Turkish Republic of Northern Cyprus carved onto the mountain slopes.

struggle. Human loyalties were flexible at best. A Turkish passport hardly enabled one to get anywhere without a visa, while a Turkish Cypriot passport got one no further than Turkey.

Practical Mehmet, like many TRNC citizens, had three passports: Turkey and TRNC, as well as the hated Republic of Cyprus, for the latter conferred visa-free privileges to Western Europe and elsewhere. The Greek government of the South, in order to assert that it was the sole legitimate government of the island, continued to issue passports to its supposed ethnic Turkish citizens in the North.

With Mehmet, we rolled across the flat Mesaoria plains south of the Kyrenian Mountains, where a large TRNC flag was carved on the mountain slopes. We stopped by Barnabas Church, whose icons have become museum exhibits after the departure of its Greek guardians.

The ancient classical city of Salamis, whose wealth attracted Alexander the Great and Cleopatra (who received it as a present from Mark Anthony), not to mention poor me, whose shoes gave way amongst the desolate ruins and lonely columns. Richard the Lionheart came as well, ravaging and plundering the island during the First Crusade, and is regarded as a murderous villain in these parts rather than the chivalrous, benevolent king of English plays and novels.

To the crusading knights, the Orthodox Christians were no different from Muslim and Jewish pagans, to be killed and plundered in the name of God. Indeed, Greek Orthodox believers still remember the Crusaders as an evil force. Pope John Paul II was visiting Athens then when we were there and local Orthodox Christians were protesting against the visit and the sacking of Constantinople 900 years ago.

In the nearby southeast Cyprus, a momentous struggle was continuing on the Asian mainland. To the Christian and Muslim Arabs of Palestine, a different crusade of sorts was continuing — Jewish warriors backed by Protestant Americans were ravaging their land and people; while the latter groups believed in their God-ordained rights to the Holiest of Lands.

We proceeded to the city of Famagusta, once the richest city on

Earth, where the dispossessed King of Jerusalem, Guy de Lusignan, feted and partied in his new capital; where Othello, the black general, ruled the great Venetian trading port and its legendary riches; and where I spent the princely-sounding sum of TL13,000,000 (US$11) on a pair of shoes.

In the 20th century, Famagusta had lived through its glorious days as the party beach of Europe. After the 1974 Turkish intervention which drove away its mainly Greek inhabitants, streets were barren and deserted. A massive ghost town of sorts stood in the southern suburbs of Famagusta, waiting for its owners to return, a long and endless wait.

From there, we rushed across the mountains to fair Kyrenia, now known as Girne. It was a pity that we did not have enough time for the quaint marina of Girne, which looked most inviting, with nice cafes and seafood restaurants gracing the quay. As we rushed back to Nicosia to beat the 5pm deadline, a gush of feelings overcame me.

These warm, friendly people had finally secured their liberty in the North, but the social costs had been heavy, for themselves as well as their enemy. Both ethnic groups had always lived across the island, but now the North was ethnically cleansed of the Greeks and the South the Turks. The old cosmopolitan, multi-racial Cyprus no longer existed. The North had become a sleepy Turkish provincial district, while the South another Greek holiday island resort. As the sun set over the bell towers and minarets of Nicosia, I mourned for a Cyprus lost forever.

Aphrodisiac in the Land of Aphrodite

After the enlightening practical lesson into the world of four-letter words, I dragged my travel companions downstairs, somewhat angry at that time, but of course, if they had been punctual, I would have missed the opportunity of capturing such wonderful writing material.

As the ancient Chinese put it, a farmer's loss of his horse could lead to both good and bad events. As the story goes, a frontier farmer lost his horse, which soon returned with another one. His son rode on the second horse, fell and broke his leg. Soon after, war broke out and because his son had an injured leg, he was not conscripted and was spared the horrors of war. So, was it a good thing that the farmer lost his horse in the first place?

We had a quick breakfast and began our exploration of Nicosia. The old city of Nicosia was not only old but also small. Ten minutes to the north and one would hit the Green Line and more pictures of bunkers and forbidden walls. It was hard to believe that within minutes of the hip shopping centres and Giorgio Armani shops, one could reach an ancient fault line of conflict and death.

We passed the Archbishop's Palace with its gigantic statue of Makarios III, the Archbishop of Cyprus and the first President of the Republic. The palace was burnt down during the 1974 *coup d'etat* against him. Missing for a few days while he sought refuge in the British military base, it was thought that he had been killed in the pro-Greek coup and that sparked off the Turkish invasion. We passed a few desolate but grand mosques, like the Barnabas Church in Northern Cyprus, which were deserted and lonely, devoid of their guardians and worshippers.

This area was once the commercial heart of old, cosmopolitan Nicosia. The events of 1974 had turned the precinct into a frontier

land, run-down and abandoned. One could close one's eyes and imagine the lively traffic, pretty ladies doing their weekend shopping, old men smoking water-pipe tobacco, teenagers going to school and tourists snapping away with their cameras; gone were the good old days. I wondered when the Cypriots would do their own version of Berlin's Potsdamerplatz rebuilding, or would they ever do it at all? Once again, I was confronted with what could have happened if Singapore had chosen the wrong route during the ethnic tension of the 1960s.

We checked out of the hotel after a fruitless attempt to book hotel rooms in Paphos, western Cyprus. We tried more than ten hotels and it appeared that nobody was interested in manning hotel receptions and when they were at the counters, they spent most of their time chatting on the telephone.

***

We bade Nicosia farewell and sped off towards the Troodos Mountains. Within an hour, we entered the uplands, where cooler weather and tall pine trees set in. We graced gently along the slopes of Mt Olympus (which island in the Greek world did not have a Mt Olympus?). It was said that the CIA had its Middle Eastern electronic surveillance centre here on the summit. Was it also on Osama's list? If Al Qaeda

Magnificent Greek– Byzantine frescoes at Kykkos Monastery on the Greek Cypriot side of the Green Line.

had cells and operatives everywhere, that global reach would certainly be matched by that of the CIA.

We stopped by a remote village along the way, had a fantastic extended meal of barbecue pork and chicken, and excellent village wine, not to mention wonderfully refreshing cool mountain spring water.

Kykkos Monastery, a World Heritage Site, was on our list (and hopefully not on Osama's). What a wonderful kaleidoscope of colours! I had a great time taking photographs of the frescoes and murals that adorned its walls. The main cathedral was amazing, too, with the gold-covered ceiling and pillars, not to mention the ancient icons and sacred relics. The Monastery Museum was also wonderful. I stood under the round museum hall with its beautiful ceiling painting of Christ the Pantokrator and tried to understand why Bruce Chatwin converted to the Orthodox Church shortly before his death. The New Age pseudo-Buddhist in me uttered a prayer in this holy spot. Is there a difference at all between the spirituality of the East and West? Are they both not different manifestations of the ultimate truth?

***

After 'stealing' a few icons (but only digital copies), we sped towards Lemesos, a large seaside city, where we loitered around the nightclub strip before retiring for the day. Russian seemed to be the third language here (after Greek and English), at least from signboards and restaurant menus. Since the collapse of the USSR, Cyprus has become the financial centre (aka 'money laundering' centre) and favourite seaside resort for the New Russians. The whole country seemed to be overwhelmed with not only Russian bankers and tourists, but also waiters and workers of the more dubious kind.

After a night in a hotel room with a balcony, we got up early the next morning, ready for a dip at the Lady's Mile beach which, according to the hotel reception, was normally full of nude ladies enjoying the sun in their full glory. This was a real aphrodisiac of sorts for my friends, who would normally have had difficulty getting up at such unholy hours. They were to be disappointed, for it was too cold to swim and nobody was around except for a few burly, hairy old men braving the cold.

We moved westwards to Paphos, passing some nice offshore rock formations which the Cypriots claimed to be the birthplace of Aphrodite, the Goddess of Love. They were pretty, but I had seen similar geographic formations elsewhere. I wondered if the local legends were 'real' Greek legends or mere tourism-inspired tales.

At Paphos, not far from the beautiful classical mosaics, we had more seafood, wine and coffee. As the sun set over the eastern edge of the Mediterranean, I dreamed of a more heroic and less complicated age, when gods and heroes battled demons and evil. Perhaps it was better to live in dreams rather than in reality, where at least the good would win most of the time and sunsets would last longer.

POSTSCRIPT:

The island of Cyprus has remained as divided as before. There were brief episodes in the last decade where it seemed probable that both sides could reach agreement on a federal state. However, opportunities have come and gone, and political parties that are most amenable towards the formation of a loose confederation and minimal reclamation of lost properties in the 1974 conflict have since lost elections on both sides of the ceasefire line.

Poland — Salt Mines, Holocaust and Phoenix Rising from Ashes (2002)

Kraków, Poland. The trumpeter's melody was soft but distinct. On the 36th note, it suddenly stopped, with the final note left unfinished. The *hejnal* was a poignant tune played from the towers of St Mary's Church, every hour on the hour, a tradition that went as far back as 1392. Legends tell of a watchman who had spied invading Mongol Tatars marching into the city and had played the trumpet to warn his fellow citizens. His warning was stopped midway when a Tatar arrow killed him, hence the abrupt ending to the tune. The warning alerted the city and saved it from destruction. Since then, a trumpeter from the city's fire service has played the melody every hour, with Polish radio playing it at noon everyday.

Poland, Land of the Brave. A nation of 38 million people, it is historically straddled between the two great powers of Europe, Germany and Russia. Its fateful location at the crossroads of two empires has shaped much of the glories as well as miseries of this nation. First founded a thousand years ago through the unity of tribes living in the plains around the Vistula River, the Polish nation united with Lithuania in 1386 when Queen Jadwiga married Grand Duke Jagiello of the Lithuanians to form what was medieval Europe's largest state, whose warriors washed their feet in both the Baltic and Black Seas and laid siege to the Kremlin in Moscow. Good times did not last. Dynastic politics led to a fragmented nation governed by foreign kings elected by a large, quarrelsome nobility (10% of the population) more interested in preserving their ancient privileges. Poland soon saw its territories crumbling into the hands of powerful neighbours and by 1795, the last of the Polish kings were deposed. Even so, the Poles never lost heart. They rebelled again and again against their powerful enemies. For indeed, as the Polish national anthem sings, "Poland has not perished yet — As long as we still live — That which foreign forces have seized — We at sword point shall retrieve."

Independence came in 1918 in the form of the Polish Republic and national fortunes were revived by Marshal Józef Pilsudski. Disaster befell the nation in 1939 when Hitler invaded, sparking the Second World War. Stalin came in from the east and divided Poland with Hitler. Hitler backstabbed his Soviet friends in 1941 by attacking them. In the ensuring war, Poland was overrun by Soviets who set up their own satellite regime. Tragic Poland lost a quarter of its population and almost its entire Jewish population in these years of war. The Polish nation rebuilt itself and began a four-decade struggle against Soviet domination. As Stalin said, turning the Poles into communists was like fitting a saddle on a cow. Victory came in 1989 when the independent trade union Solidarity defeated the communists in the first-ever free elections, thus sparking off democratic revolutions across Eastern Europe, eventually leading to the toppling of the Soviet Union itself.

Since then, Poland has undergone an economic transformation towards capitalism and joined the European Union on 1 May 2004. At last, Poland, the country that gave the world Chopin, Mrs Curie (Maria Sklodowska-Curie) and Copernicus, was back at the heart of Central Europe (they find the description 'Eastern Europe' offensive). With almost equal voting rights as Germany in the Council of Ministers of Europe (27 vs. Germany's 29), Poland soon emerged as a new European power. History, it seemed, had come full circle.

I arrived in Warsaw on a Friday night. Loud bright neon lights glowed into a city sky crowded with shiny new office towers and massive shopping malls. Pepsi, Sanyo, Citibank, Pierre Cardin,

McDonald's and so on — was I in an American city? Only the massive 30 hectare square (and 3,288-room), 231-metre tall Soviet-built Palace of Culture and Science, built in what could be described as a Soviet Baroque birthday cake style size XXX, reminded one that this was once a Central European junction behind the Iron Curtain. These days, banners proclaiming the glories of *Newsweek* and a local supermarket chain hung from what used to be the citadel of communism where slogans devoted to the Working Class once hung. Stalin would have turned in his grave.

Hotel Warszawa, a hotel built in the old Soviet days, was my port of call. Whereas many new international chain hotels with flashy glass panels have appeared in Warsaw, Hotel Warszawa with its neo-classical columns and faded colours seemed to be an under-invested remnant of the past, the only difference being the front desk *babushkas* who spoke fairly good English (in fact, it seemed that many people below the age of 40 spoke fairly good English in this country). A dusty red carpet sprawled across the corridor and a worn-out chandelier reminded one of better times past. Five flyers on a drawing table with glossy prints of half-dressed ladies greeted me as I stepped out of the lift. "Beautiful Ladies for You — Many Handsome Men Too — Guarantee Arrival Within 10 Minutes of Order." To be fair, there are more of such sleazy flyers around everywhere in London, but that is new capitalism for you!

The plains of Mazovia where the Polish cavalry once charged against German tanks.

Saturday was a day of cobbled streets and salt mines. We woke up early to take the train to Kraków. (Only one flyer remained on the drawing table by morning, indicating the takeup rate of the enticing offer the night before.) Within minutes, the Tatry Express sped across the flat fertile plains of Mazovia, the region in Central Poland where Warsaw reigned. I was reminded of those brave Polish cavalrymen with their lancers who charged fearlessly, perhaps foolishly, across these plains at the invading German tanks in the first days of the war. Their Air Force counterparts later displayed numerous feats of courage in the Battle of Britain, including other Polish forces in Monte Cassino, Tobruk, Normandy and so on. Such battles have long characterised the Polish desire for freedom and their willingness to die for the national cause.

Before long, the plains gave way to small green fields occasionally punctuated by little wooded hills somewhat resembling the well-proportioned breasts of a young woman. Now brightened by orange autumn foliage, the region, known as Malopolska, or Little Poland, rose gradually to the Carpathian Mountains on the southern borders with Slovakia. If Poland once began in Wielkopolska (or Great Poland) just west of Warsaw, it was in Malopolska that it matured and blossomed. This was the very spiritual heart of Poland, where the kings reigned, where the future Pope John Paul II once lived, and where great composers wrote songs for the rest of the world. Kraków, the capital of Poland for half a millennia until 1569, was at the heart of Malopolska and the very epicentre of Polish conscience and culture.

It took two and half hours to reach Kraków, where I dropped my luggage at Jordan Guesthouse, a brand new set-up with IKEA-style furniture and a cool glass lift. I then headed for Market Square in the old town. Cobbled streets, forbidding towers with huge venerable bells, cathedrals with bright yellow stars in royal blue ceilings, ancient merchant houses turned fashionable bars, cyber-stations in medieval courtyards and cafes al fresco where one could sit for hours watching beautiful people walking past. This was Kraków, the new

Prague, minus the tourist crowds. It was difficult not to fall in love with beautiful and hip Kraków.

I wandered around the streets and then popped by Wawel, a walled city within the Old City. Here within its confines were the Royal Palace and Wawel Cathedral. I explored the latter's crypts and its royal tombs — this was the Polish equivalent of Westminster Abbey — where the prominent in Polish history were buried. I climbed the tower of the cathedral with a crowd of cheerful Russian *babushkas* and helped a few to take shots from the tall Sigismund Tower, just above a cross commemorating the Khatyn Massacre of 1940, when Soviet forces executed 15,000 Polish officers in the forests of Belarus.

Just east of Wawel was the Kazimierz district, the old Jewish quarter of Kraków. Jews used to account for 22% of the population of Kraków. Hitler's Final Solution destroyed the 800 years of Jewish heritage in Kraków, although Oscar Schindler, the famous Nazi businessman, managed to rescue some of the Kraków Jews by putting them on his payroll. I decided to skip his factory a few kilometres to the east, now part of the newly commercialised *Schindler's List* trail. Instead, I explored Kazimierz and its neglected, dilapidated streets. A few synagogues remained, but they were all closed on the Sabbath. After a quick examination of a flashy restaurant cum bookshop (a strange combination) loudly proclaiming 'Jewish Cuisine, Live Jewish Music', I hopped into a taxi and headed to the bus station.

I made my way to the Royal Salt Mines of Wieliczka which, like the old town of Kraków, was a World Heritage Site. Here, over a few hundred years, miners had created an underground museum of art, with whole halls and chapels carved from rock and salt, complete with chandeliers and statues large and small. An amazing feat of art, apart from those chapels and halls, were quite a few scattered sculptures of dwarfs and legends which had somewhat turned this complex into an over-glorified underground theme park.

Sunday was the day of death. I walked in soft, gentle rain to the Church of the Reformed Franciscans, where the unusual combination of underground air and minerals had preserved the bodies of 18th century monks. I had hesitated about coming here but the irresistible temptation of viewing the macabre prevailed. The crypt would not open until later in the day, said the handsome young Franciscan monk whom I approached, and that solved my dilemma. In any case, I had had enough of mummies, having visited one too many Capuchin and Franciscan crypts full of mummified monks. I often wondered why natural mummification seemed to happen more frequently to members of these orders. A divine protection or curse?

Auschwitz, the Nazi death camp, was next. 'Arbeit Macht Frei' or 'Work Makes Free', read the cynical sign across the entrance of the camp. Here, between 1941 and 1945, 1.7 million people perished — 70% of them Jews, the rest being Poles, Russians, Yugoslavs, Gypsies, homosexuals and any other group whom the Nazis considered disagreeable. There were electrified barbed wires (which became a suicide aid for many camp detainees), watch-towers and signposts with skull and crossbones.

This was a grim place on a grim day. The skies were grey and the winds were howling, not to mention the intermittent rain. A fitting atmosphere for a visit to a place where terrible things had happened. I had been to Dachau Concentration Camp in Germany, but that was on a much smaller scale compared to Auschwitz.

Nothing needed to be explained when one saw an enormous glass case half the size of a large room full of hair from women killed in the gas chambers. These had been removed from victims' heads to be mixed with linen for the manufacturing of cloth. There were also thousands of toothbrushes displayed in a similar glass case, personal belongings of the dead harvested for reuse elsewhere in the Reich, and luggage bags with the names and addresses of the dead scribbled on them; the victims had been told they would be resettled in the East and had therefore made sure that their luggage had been carefully labelled. There were thousands of artificial limbs — even these were deemed harvestable from the victims. Then the tales of the courageous:

the Polish lady who had passed food to the detainees and had been sent to the death camps as well; Father Kolbe who was later canonised: he offered to take the place of a man who had been selected for execution due to the escape of some detainees.

Three kilometres away was Birkenau Camp, also known as Auschwitz II. The gas chambers were tested and perfected in Auschwitz I, but it was at Birkenau that a full factory production line of death was built. Huge gas chambers were located just next to the railway station. Doctors of death made casual visual examinations of the newly arrived and then divided them into those who could work and those who could not. The former were made to work to their death, while the latter were simply and immediately dispatched into the gas chambers and told to undress so that they could bathe. In reality, cyanide was filtered into the chambers. At its peak, 60,000 people a day were 'processed' in this camp.

As I left the town of Oswiecim, which was the actual Polish name of the town which the Nazis had Germanised as Auschwitz, I was reminded of the famous quotation, "If we do not remember history, we are condemned to repeat it." Winds howled as storms beat down upon the fading, run-down houses of Oswiecim. As a side note, I pitied the people of this town, their name forever associated with these infamous factories of death. It had to be difficult for town officials to

Beautiful old Kraków.

encourage any form of investment. I could not see businesses wanting to have that name on their business addresses. Although the Polish name sounded somewhat different from the German one, it was nonetheless difficult to see Oswiecim as an auspicious place.

Back to Kraków, I had coffee and cake at a classical, turn-of-the-19th-century artists' café called Jama Michalika, surrounded by stylish décor and old paintings, with prices no higher than a normal London café. As rain poured outside on the cobbled streets of Kraków, I dreamt of times past while looking at beautiful young people as I enjoyed the last hours of Sunday.

Monday was the day of the phoenix rising from the ashes. I left beautiful Kraków by rail and travelled back to Warsaw. The capital of Poland since the union with Lithuania, Warsaw was a city of 1.7 million people and many palaces, not just of kings but also of the many members of nobility that once dominated the country. After all, this was once a royal republic, where kings were elected, thus allowing foreign powers the opportunity of interfering in its domestic politics by supporting their preferred candidates and manipulating the votes. As a result, foreigners were often elected kings rather than the Poles. What was worse was the atrociously democratic system called *liberum veto*, through which members of parliament (the Sejm) had the right to veto any bill, to dissolve the Sejm and even to annul previous decisions. This was applied very often in the 17th and 18th centuries, thus paralysing governance of the country, leading to its decline and then partition of Poland by neighbouring powers.

The Palace of Culture and Science aside, buildings of monumental proportions, statues and sculptures were visible everywhere. These masked the fact that more than 90% of Warsaw was destroyed during World War II. When the westward marching Soviet Army reached the east bank of the Vistula River, Warsaw rose up in revolt against the Germans. The Soviets, apprehensive about the non-communist insurgents controlling Warsaw, refused to assist in the uprising, thus allowing the Germans to crush it with all their might. The city was bombed, shelled and blown to bits even after the surrender of the insurgents. There were moving memorials of these brave insurgents abound in the city. In many street corners where civilians were massacred, one could find memorials to the dead. In the heart of the Old City was a particularly poignant one, that of the Little Insurgent, a bronze sculpture of a child carrying a rifle. I walked around the old town and its pretty merchant houses, marvelled at the extent to which the Poles have rebuilt their capital wholesale after the war, so much so that the old town has been declared a UNESCO World Heritage site.

I explored the Warsaw Ghetto just north of the old town, where half a million Jews were holed up by the Germans during the war, many later deported to the death camps and the remaining slaughtered during the uprising. An Israeli group complete with the Star-of-David flag congregated at the site of the last bunker of the Jewish Resistance Army (which fought alongside the Polish Home Army against the Nazis), holding prayers for the dead. Gentle rain dropped as they prayed while I wondered if it was the Palestinians who were now paying the price for Hitler's atrocities. An injured Afghan boy grinned straight from the frontpage of local newspapers. Perhaps heaven was weeping for the atrocities mankind had brought upon itself, not just the last World War and subsequent conflicts, but also of the terrible

things that all sides in the conflict had done to civilians who often had nothing to do with the decisions taken by politicians, but yet had to bear the brunt of it all.

POSTSCRIPT:

Since joining the European Union in 2004, Poland has experienced enormous economic growth. In fact, Poland is the only EU member that has continued to grow its economy despite the global financial crisis of the past few years. New-found wealth has also allowed the Polish people to travel extensively, and I have met Polish travellers even in remote parts of Africa and Asia over the past few years.

AFRICA / INDIAN OCEAN

INDIAN
OCEAN

● **MADAGASCAR**

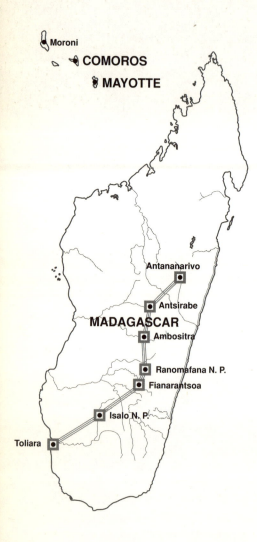

N

Moroni

COMOROS

MAYOTTE

Antananarivo

Antsirabe

MADAGASCAR

Ambositra

Ranomafana N. P.

Fianarantsoa

Isalo N. P.

Toliara

MAURITIUS

Port Louis

Saint Denis

RÉUNION

Mauritius — Globalisation, Life & Death in the Land of the Dodo (2003)

As dead as a dodo. This is a bird that once lived in Mauritius — a fat, clumsy giant cousin of the modern-day pigeon that had a strange awkward-shaped beak and could not fly. It once thrived on this island that forms the remains of an extinct volcano at the lower end of the Indian Ocean, where pure precinct isolation protected the flightless bird from the ravages of larger predators. However, after the arrival of man in the 17th century, the bird was hunted to extinction, and its eggs devoured by dogs, cats and pigs brought here by their human masters.

One might be tempted to blame the Dutch sailors, although contemporary accounts said that the dodo tasted disgusting, but who could blame these sailors who had spent half a year on the sea from Europe and would have tasted nothing but half decomposed turtle and sick chickens? Whatever it is, today, the dodo — or rather, skeletal remains of this once magnificently ugly bird — is only found in museums. In Mauritius, the dodo has become a national symbol. Around the world, it has become the byword for extinction, or dead, dead silence.

Port Louis, the capital of Mauritius, is quiet on a Sunday, not quite as dead as a dodo but not significantly more. There was hardly any soul in sight. A watchman sweeping the entrance to the ornate mosque with a lotus pool in its inner compound; an elderly Chinese hawker selling *yong tau fu* (a category of delicious dumplings the Hakka people of southern China are famous for); vendors arriving and setting up stalls in the nearby market. This is a small city at the head of a sheltered bay, hammered in by the mountains.

***

Mauritius — named after Maurice, the Prince of Orange and leader of the United Dutch Provinces. At 1865 sq km, this is an island three times the size of Singapore but with only 1.2 million people. The friendly Mauritians tend to complain about how crowded their island is, but I can only wish Singapore was larger, and equally endowed with wild green mountains, mysterious unfathomable forests, ocean-beating cliffs, fine sandy beaches and pretty tropical coral atolls. Maybe I am asking for too much, for Mauritius is often equated with paradise.

This is land of the sugar cane — 80% of all cultivated land is covered by sugar cane plantations and 25% of all export earnings is derived from sugar. As one drives across the island, the roads pass through endless horizons of sugar cane, singing Bihari peasants and an occasional Creole mansion. It was the Dutch who first introduced the crop to this island and in no time sugar cane had covered the entire island.

Port Louis from the sky.

The French intensified the cultivation of sugar cane and the local French aristocracy grew enormously wealthy from it. They built palatial mansions in their enormous estates across the island, and held grand parties and festivities. When the British Navy arrived during the Napoleonic War, these 'Grand Blanc' (or 'Great Whites') surrendered quickly to the British, on the condition that they were allowed to run the economy and practice their religion and customs in the same way as before.

The sugar barons, as this wealthy class is known, continue to control the Mauritian economy today. The Franco-Mauritian community comprises of about 1% of the population, but most of the wealth. 51 of the top 100 Chief Executives in Mauritius are Franco-Mauritians, and five of their top families control 18 of the top 50 companies in the country. This is a country with a GDP per capita of US$3,800[1] and most of the wealth is highly concentrated within this very small group of people.

In 1968, just before independence, riots broke out between the Creoles and Muslims. "The government announced that only 4 died but we all knew that it was more than 100, courtesy of BBC," said a senior Franco-Mauritian banker. "And most of my relatives emigrated to France, South Africa, Australia." The rest stayed on and the old lifestyle continued. The rules of the game since then are, the Indian-Mauritians will run the government and civil service while the Franco-Mauritians keep the economy and their wealth. As for the Creoles, well...

***

This is a fertile land midway between the tropics and temperate. Many types of fruits can be grown here — both tropical and temperate ones, including strawberries, papayas, bananas, melons and pineapples. However, many of them do not seem very tasty or large. Perhaps this

---

[1] By 2009, the GDP per capita (PPP) of Mauritius would be US$12,526 (and $6,838 on nominal basis).

is the case of a Jack-of-all-trades and master of none. What this island grows well is sugar cane. Unfortunately, they don't drink sugar cane juice, which Southeast Asians love. Here, they export everything.

***

I stayed at Labourdonnais Waterfront, the top business hotel in Port Louis. The Waterfront area is the most modern and chic area in the capital. The rest of the capital is fairly dilapidated apart from the glass tower-headquarters of a few local banks and financial institutions. Mauritius aspires to be the regional financial centre of the Indian Ocean rim, but post-Apartheid South Africa is the real powerhouse of Africa. Who needs to do banking in Mauritius?

Small nations like Mauritius and Singapore provide refuge for capital when larger neighbours are less advanced, or in political trouble, but when order is restored, the money moves away if there is no special reason to remain. We all have to find our niche and survive. Both Mauritius and Singapore face the same challenges.

Mauritius tells the world that it is part of Africa, and Africa's bridge to the world, but the reality is somewhat different.

"We don't really know Africa well. We went in and were cheated by the Mozambiqueans, Malagasy and so on. We don't do business the same way they do. But if we don't move in, where do we go from this side of the Indian Ocean?" said another senior banker.

I am reminded of Singapore's own experience in dealing with China, Vietnam, and the rest of Asia. We are Asians and yet we aren't. We think we know the region well, but we have a lot to learn, and are paying very high school fees to learn from our mistakes.

Transparency International rates Mauritius as one of the least corrupt countries in Africa, after Botswana and Seychelles. However, this is nothing is celebrate about, for African standards of public and corporate governance are hardly impressive by world standards. Everyone here knows the intertwining strings of influence and money in this country, and how the tiny group of elite and politicians pat each other's back.

***

Mauritius is a member of the Commonwealth of Nations (i.e. an organisation of former British colonies who have decided to come together for the poorer countries to beg for some cash from the richer ones, and for the Brits to relive the long-past glories of the Empire in a painless manner) and so I thought they might be very English. In fact, I was surprised to find how French this island is.

The locals speak Creole at home and French at work. English, however, is the language of public signboards and documentation. The premier local business periodical, *Business Magazine*, has an English title and French content. There are a few French language daily papers but only one weekly in English, titled *News on Sunday*. *News on Sunday*, which has screaming tabloid-like headlines on Beckham and the latest Miss South Africa, is on sale on Friday and usually sold out by Saturday.

People here — the well-to-do ones, that is — still send their

Port Louis' Chinatown.

children to France for studies, although there is an increasing trend for people to go to Australia.

There is French cable TV soft porn on Fridays and Saturdays. Once, while fast scanning the hotel TV, I stumbled onto a bizarre Chinese porno dubbed in French, and it had people wearing costumes from obviously wrong historical periods. Of course, costume authenticity is not critical in movies where the objective is to get rid of clothing as quickly as possible.

***

Port Louis has a Chinatown. Here it was quiet, dilapidated and dirty. Like Chinatowns elsewhere, it had traditional Chinese gateways. A few street hawkers and rugged stray dogs greeted the visitor. There were a few Chinese restaurants too, but the best Chinese restaurants have moved to the suburbs.

Mauritius has over 30,000 Chinese, descendants of Hakka traders. Today, they are scattered throughout the island but many have remained in Port Louis and its surrounding areas. Isolated from the mainstream Chinese-speaking world, the Sino-Mauritians are relatively integrated within Mauritian society. They are more comfortable speaking Creole and French, than Mandarin and Hakka. As a Chinese street hawker told me, "We have lost our roots."

All human beings are prisoners of history. Sino-Mauritians have names in formats which are unfamiliar to most ethnic Chinese worldwide. The full name of first generation Sino-Mauritians often became the surname of his descendants. Take for example, somebody called Jean-Claude Yong Shing Fook. Note the French first name, Jean-Claude: this is a guy — Jean is a masculine name in French. His surname is Yong Shing Fook, for that is the full name of his great grandfather who emigrated from Guangdong Province, China, in the 1920s. Yong was obviously the surname of his great grandpa and Shing Fook the 'first name'. However, colonial bureaucrats in Mauritius in those days had decided that this was their preferred format for names. And so all of Monsieur Yong's descendants would have to be known not as Monsieur Yong but Monsieur Yong Shing Fook.

In any case, some supposedly Chinese traits have remained. I have met a number of well-educated local Sino-Mauritians, many of them holding important positions in the financial sector. Chinese, as usual, are good at numbers and technical things and hence they basically run the finance and accounting departments of a large local bank, as well as anything that requires familiarity with numbers. The Franco-Mauritians and Indo-Mauritians tend to score better in marketing and group leadership, and thus run a lot of major operations — in fact they hold the most important positions in the banks. (Of course, it is the Franco-Mauritians who actually own everything!) The Creoles (descendants of African slaves) generally do less well in schools, and many do manual work.

***

There is no *Harry Potter* fever in Mauritius. You can walk in and buy the book off the shelf. I'm not entirely sure if Mauritians read a lot — Mauritius ranks 67th in the Human Development Index and 2nd in Africa.[2] The local bookshops are few and small. I don't know what they do after dark. Everything closes at 5pm — including restaurants and bars (apart from those in hotels and on the Waterfront). Perhaps they all go home and watch TV or make babies?

***

Manufacturing is the second pillar of the Mauritian economy (followed by tourism and finance). The heart of Mauritian industry is the Export Processing Zone (EPZ). Since the 1980s, Mauritius has provided incentives for foreign manufacturers. This has led to massive investment

---

[2] By 2009, Mauritius ranked 81st and 3rd in worldwide and African HDI respectively.

by Hong Kong textile manufacturers seeking to take advantage of unutilised textile quotas Mauritius has with major Western economies. HK investment in the EPZ has increased employment significantly in Mauritius and created a second pillar to the previously largely agricultural nature of the local economy.

16% of the nation's workforce work for the EPZ, 80% of which are in the textile industry, which contributes to 20% of the Mauritian GDP. Mauritius, a warm subtropical island, has suddenly become the largest exporter of woolen knitters in the world. However, these investors soon realised that Mauritians were somewhat less productive than workers in China, and this led to a bizarre development — Mainland Chinese workers were flown into Mauritius to work in these HK-owned factories — which had already used up both HK and China's textile quotas with EU and USA — to supplement the less productive local workforce.

The EPZ, however, is now in deep crisis. China is now in the World Trade Organization and much of the previous textile quotas has been lifted. With China's enormous industry capacity and cheap but highly skilled and productive workforce, there is no more reason for Hong Kong manufacturers to fly Mainland Chinese workers to far-flung factories in Mauritius, Guatemala and Honduras. As Mauritian subcontractors have not upgraded their skills and equipment since

Sugar plantation, Mauritius.

the good old days, they find their costs high and sales revenue dropping. One by one, the foreign investors leave, and factories close.

The process is continuing. The story is not new. Mauritius has to find its niches fast, just as Singapore faces the same challenge. Yet another anecdote in our increasingly globalised world.

***

Last week, CNN aired a report about the plight of Diego Garcia, the largest island atoll in the world, right in the heart of the Indian Ocean. This island was once ruled by the British from Mauritius but was detached to become a separate colony in 1965, known as the British Indian Ocean Territory (although Mauritius retained an official claim on it). In 1972, more than 2000 inhabitants of the island were forcibly removed to Mauritius so as to facilitate the building of one of the largest air bases in the world by the United States.

Today, the islanders of Diego Garcia languish in the slums of Port Louis, dreaming about their island paradise, of that idyllic lifestyle, fishing, birds and everything that comes with it. Many among them have no jobs and suffer from chronic alcoholism and depression. Suicide rates are also high. CNN describes their removal as moving 'from Paradise to Hell'. In 2000, they won a lawsuit in London against the British Government for the terrible injustice they suffered. However, the judgment stopped short of deciding whether they should be allowed to return to their homeland. An injustice on an entire people carried out by a democratic country in such recent times.

The islanders asked if they could visit their ancestral graves, but the British told them that they would have to ask the Americans. When the islanders approached the US State Department, they received a polite letter about how critical the islands are to the Fight Against Terrorism, and that since the islands are nominally British territory, the islanders should ask the British Government instead. And so the saga continues for the Diego Garcia islanders.

***

The hotel placed a copy of an African business magazine, *Traders — African Business Journal*, under my door. It's a very interesting magazine. The main article announces: 'Business Opportunities Blossom in DRC & Angola following peace initiatives'. It shows a picture of a sunflower bursting out of a pistol. Unfortunately, to the left of the pistol is the header of another article, 'Corporate Governance — A Return To African Values'.

One of the key articles is an interview with President Joseph Kabila of the Democratic Republic of Congo (DRC), in which he invited investors to DRC, and spoke about the wonderful opportunities in the tourism, hydroelectric power and mining sectors. Well, I guess he forgot to tell you that one of the worst civil wars ever fought in the world in the last five decades is still ongoing in the country, and that he barely controls half of his country.

***

After a month on the project, we finally had a chance to go to the beach (just for one night). We hopped into two taxis and headed for Le St Géran, a luxury resort that charges a ridiculous sum of money per night. The place was named after a 18th century sinking ship which carried a stubborn girl, Virginie, who refused to remove her bulky formal dress to swim ashore and drowned in the open seas nearby as a result, thus inspiring the famous story, Paul & Virginie.

What a scandal — Wee Cheng going to a bourgeois resort and dining in an Alain Ducasse restaurant? (Alain Ducasse is a Michelin three-star French celebrity chef who gives fanciful names to the dishes and charges silly diners for the privilege.) Well, every dog has its day, doesn't it? At least, I have learnt that luxury resorts aren't for me. I missed the smell and sounds of local markets; the Bohemian atmosphere of a local writer's café; the most exotic street food with flies and maggots; or really bad crowded buses with all the chickens on your lap.

I got into a paddleboat and tried to reach the Hindu temple on the other side of the cove. Instead, the strong currents brought me to the beach. Only my frantic paddling efforts finally brought me back to the sheltered safety of the inner cove. It's like an hour-long intensive cycling session in the gym — the only difference being that it wasn't a session I could stop if I wanted to. I might even reach Australia or Sumatra if the currents were strong enough, perhaps?

***

Enough of work, work, work. I got into a rented car with Adrian, a Dutch traveller I got to know on the *Lonely Planet* bulletin board while discussing Madagascar. We hit it off right away after meeting for drinks on a Friday night — two nomads bumping into each other in the middle of nowhere, and we rolled off the names of places like Burkina Faso, Mogadishu, Transdniestria and Ulaanbaatar as though they were neighbourhood lanes — and he invited me to join him in his rented car to explore the south and southeast of this country.

On Saturday morning, Adrian picked me up in Port Louis and we drove to the quiet fishing town of Mahébourg. This is the oldest political centre in the country, near where the Dutch first landed in 1598. We

A spectacular view of the Lion's Mountain, Vieux Grand Port.

strolled along the fading streets of this town of wooden houses under the shadow of coconut and palm trees, and had coffee and a no-frills eggs and butter cake in a small Indian shop.

Mahébourg is simple and thoroughly sleepy. Apart from a Chinese takeaway shop and a half-constructed Chinese casino, it is anything but cosmopolitan. In fact, with all the flowing exuberance of the Indian *saris* and the aromatic smell of incense from smallish Hindu shrines, this place looks like a provincial Indian village, with English and occasionally French signboards.

It was also here in the Vieux Grand Port (Great Old Port), under the soaring heights of the Lion Mountain, that the French Navy scored their only naval victory against the British in the Napoleonic Wars, the Battle of Mahébourg, which was inscribed on the marble walls of the Triumphant Arch in Paris. Now, only the gentle sails of fishing boats break the silence of this bay of small islets.

We drove on the coastal road, past rows of huge casuarinas — where you can almost imagine Bollywood musicals been filmed — and endless acres of sugar cane plantations. We passed small fishing villages along the coastal fringes of the lion-headed Lion Mountain, with names such as Ville Noire, Riviere des Creoles, Vieux Grand Port, Boix des Amourettes and Providence.

We bashed through the narrow, sometimes muddy tracks of deep sugar plantations, testing the suspension limits of our pathetic little Peugeot. After travelling up and down small hills and we found ourselves in a ylang ylang estate. In the shaded restaurant of the estate overlooking a green valley of sugar cane and ylang ylang, we had Creole chicken and prawn for lunch. The proprietors, unfortunately, had run out of venison, the specialty of the area. Deers were first introduced by French governors anxious to bring to this island the fine traditions of hunting at Royal Court of Versailles. The dodo were long dead by then and introduced species such as goats, dogs, cats and cows were rapidly transforming the eco-environment of this island.

Onwards to Domaine du Chasseur, an even more distinguished estate once ruled by the French sugar barons. Here one can still partake in boar and deer hunting, feasting on venison cooked in *chasseur* (aka fresh deer blood), or jungle walking while living in elaborate lodges built by entrepreneurial descendants of the sugar kings, who realised that they could make more money from tourism than good old sugar.

We then took a drive around the dirt tracks, followed by a 30-minute climb up a hill with beautiful palm-trees ravaged by the strange but equally pretty nests of weaving birds, such that they looked like jesters' hats. On the top of the hill was the estate bar, with an incredibly panoramic view of the hills and deep sugar cane valleys of the eastern part of this island. This is the place to bring someone special and watch magnificent sunsets over the Indian Ocean.

On Sunday, we sped southwards through deep sugar cane plantations. We dropped by an old French sugar baron's pretty palatial Creole mansion. It was Sunday, the day of rest, when the baron's descendants had gone to church. Outside the iron gates of *fleur-de-lis* grills, we could almost imagine the baron having a mid morning tryst with his pretty black slave girl from Madagascar, with loud passionate moaning in the subtropical heat. As usual, when the pregnant girl became too large to fit her dress, the baroness would send her to a remote corner of the estate, a place full of girls of a similar fate, with

The Ganges of Mauritius: Sunset at the Hindu temple at Grand Bassion.

their mixed blood children, forgotten but forerunners of a new race — the Creoles of the paradise isles of Indian Ocean; the by-products of global cultural exchange and trading servitude. Of course, the baroness wouldn't be happy, but a new tailored evening gown delivered on the latest boat from London, and a diamond ring from Antwerp would help. So, life went on in this timeless, isolated isle at the far southern end of the Indian Ocean.

The Indian Ocean... huge waves beat the wild rugged cliffs — including one named in honour of black magic — on the southern coast of this island. Families picnicked on viewpoints while lovers hugged each other at quieter pathways along the precarious cliff sides. Brave fishermen trying their luck on boulders barely metres from the giant waves. Nothing lies between here and Antarctica. Can you hear the cry of penguins beyond the great ocean?

We tried looking for the Rochester Falls, but got lost in an enormous sugar cane plantation instead. (Perhaps we were near The Thames, with Dover nearby, and The Hague should be just across the drain?) We drove along the coast, passing dilapidated villages and quaint towns where shops are sometimes known simply as The General Store. We passed Hindu temples, a Muslim funeral, Catholic churches, secret coves of white sand and rows of coconut trees leading to paradise. Yes, and a quiet Muslim town named Surinam (oh, where is the Guyana border?) boasted a loud Hindi video shop, a Patisserie Iran

with nice Dutch cakes, and where we had wonderful fried rice in a cafe which served nothing but the one dish. Satisfied, we turned inland to the soaring greenish-black mountains.

Land of Coloured Earth — that was the first tourist trap of the day, a forest clearing with soil of shades of red, brown and orange. I bet that's what you would get if you excavate Trafalgar Square. More worthy was the Chamarel Falls nearby, the tallest in this country. The flat central plateau plunged 100 metres here, a spectacular sight in that sea of endless greenery.

Heading further inland, we entered the Black River Gorges National Park, a well-forested area with panoramic views of misty mountains, deep river valleys and the bright blue ocean at the very horizon. The park was full of visitors in their convoys of cars: urbanites looking for a weekend of family fun, not so much admiring the natural scenery, but more participating in the national sport — plucking the reddish China guavas, like Russians going for mushroom picking. I don't know which I disliked more — excited locals destroying their own country's natural flora by plucking the fruits, or partying with loud Hindi music amidst nature's gift to this island?

We drove towards the national motorway and enjoyed the sunset at a sacred Hindu lake — the Indians believe that Shiva was cruising around in heavens with River Ganges on his head, when he sprayed a few water droplets of the holy river onto this island by mistake, thus creating a crater lake. The Ganges protested the loss of such holy water but Shiva assured that in years to come, devotees of the river would pay homage to the gods from this lake, as faraway as it might be from Mother India.

Indeed, the Indians here have built a temple on the banks of this tiny lake, which they believe to be the equivalent of the Holy River, and where they worship their gods and protect the sacred fish. As sun set over this strange temple next to a strange lake on a strange island, we wondered about peace and spiritual harmony in this increasingly chaotic world where the large fish swallow the small ones whole.

And with that, we drove towards Port Louis. Another day on this beautiful island in the middle of nowhere.

POSTSCRIPT:

The Mauritian economy has continued to evolve. The textile industry has become less important to the country. By 2010, textile only contributes 6.5% of the nation's GDP, a significant drop from the levels at the time of my visit in 2003. But offshore banking and financial services, largely those linked to India, have emerged as a significant sector of the economy, contributing 12% of the economy. The rise of India as an economic power has benefited Mauritius, as much as the rise of China has benefited economies such as Hong Kong and Singapore.

Comoros — Volcano, Decay and Illusions in the Islands of the Moon
(2003)

Comoros — the Islands of the Moon in the Arabic language. Although the name is romantic, the Comoros (an archipelago of four large islands located halfway between the coast of East Africa and the northern tip of the island of Madagascar) has had a most unsavoury reputation in the last three decades. With 600,000 people squeezed into 2,170km^2, the Comoros is a very small and crowded island chain, with perhaps more coups per year than any other country in the world.

Since its independence from France in 1975, no less than 20 successful coups or attempted *coups d'etat* have occurred, with the first coup occurring less than one month after its independence. The first two presidents were brutally killed in coups and South Africa-backed white mercenaries ruled the country behind the presidential throne for much of the 1970s and 1980s. Political and natural disasters continue to plague the country to this very day.

***

"Welcome to a five-star resort!" I told E, jokingly of course, as our plane landed in the tiny international airport of Moroni, the ramshackle capital of a desperately poor Comoros, located in the nation's largest island — Grande Comore. Taxi drivers and touts surrounded us as we stepped into the arrival room (note my avoidance of the word 'hall') of the terminal building, its inner walls unpainted and covered with an amazing kaleidoscope of spider webs. Even at this point, we had neither collected our luggage nor gone through passport controls. Welcome to chaos!

Anyone could enter the Comoros. One simply queued behind a passport check counter (or just walked around it) to get one's passport stamped by a bored official who inked it without even the slightest glance at you. They had probably figured out that things were so bad there that no one would want to come and stay illegally anyway. One only needed to pay them a visa fee of about 6 euros before leaving the country.

Just as we struggled through the masses of unwelcome touts after getting our passports stamped, loud vibrant beats of drums followed by the clucking of tongues and high pitched shrieks were heard coming from the entrance of the building. A crowd of over 20 Comorian women, dressed in their finest, refreshingly colourful and almost flamboyant national costumes, were screaming their heads off as a tall Comorian man in formal shirt and tie stepped into view, smiling and waving his arms at an admiring crowd. The drums rolled further and a hysterical-looking lady stepped forward, heaping praises (or so I thought) on this handsome young man — possibly in his mid-30s — who had flown from Paris via Seychelles, with his wife and baby son. The rest clapped loudly, obviously approving the gesture, while other women in conservative *burqa* preferred to watch from a far corner with their aristocratic husbands in flowing Arab robes, betraying the partial Middle Eastern heritage of these islands.

"A singer," murmured a man who stood near me.

As I was happily snapping away with my camera, a huge pot-bellied white man waved at me. "Wee Cheng? I'm Michel from Villa Jessica. Welcome to Comoros!"

I had been in touch earlier with Michel's wife, Cécile, on the Internet. This charming French couple rented out rooms in their pretty mansion in Moroni for a reasonable rate. Most importantly, they spoke English. There were no English guidebooks available about the Comoros and I felt that it was important to stay at a place where I could find out more about what to do and see.

Michel and his Comorian driver helped us with our luggage, and then got us into his rather battle-worn car. As we drove away stirring a snowball of dust behind us, I pointed to the celebratory crowd still at the terminal building, "Singer?"

"What singer? Just another guy who has washed toilets in Marseilles for ten years and is now returning home for a visit. He's going to spend all his savings in one week, giving presents and throwing a party for everyone he knows and doesn't know. His relatives and friends are here to welcome the arrival of the money machine!"

"This is the Comoros. I have been here for 37 years, witnessed 17 out of 20-odd coups and this country has seen nothing but decline, year after year! A hundred thousand people — one-sixth of the population — live in France, and if not for the remittances of these French-Comorians and international aid, the people living here would have starved to death!"

He went on and on as we drove southwards along the pothole-riddled road to Moroni, under the tropical shade of coconuts and travellers' palms, passing an occasional village of dilapidated houses made of dried mud walls and aluminium sheet roofs.

To the far left was Karthala Volcano, all of 2,361m in height, with the largest active crater in the world — three by four kilometres in dimension — rising high up above the thick canopy of tropical jungle. In fact, the entire island of Grande Comore is a gigantic volcano which rises from the deep ocean. It slopes more gently on its western side to form the narrow coastal strip, home to most of the island's inhabitants. Karthala dominates the entire isle and you can see it everywhere on Grande Comore.

Pointing to the smoke and dust covering the dome of the volcano, Michel said, "Look at Karthala. All that smoke appearing in the past few weeks. Seismic activity has increased significantly these past few days. French scientists monitoring it say Karthala is going to erupt anytime, and the French Embassy has issued an alert."

"What?" I could not believe my ears.

"Yes, that's what they say. Karthala erupts every ten to twenty years and a village or two gets destroyed. That's nothing if you have 20 coups in 28 years."

I could only grin. In any case, the next flight was two days away and we could only hope that the volcano did not erupt before then or we would not have been able to get out.

"Don't worry, my friends. Leave everything in the hands of Allah, the Comorians will tell you. If the volcano doesn't get you, the next coup might. So why worry so much!" Michel laughed. "I'm more worried if you don't get electricity today. Electricity has been off the past two weeks now that only one of the six power stations was operating."

Before long, we were in the dilapidated centre of Moroni and amidst its messy traffic. Michel's driver negotiated smartly around the chaos and we arrived at Villa Jessica, a pretty mansion with a cosy garden of exotic tropical plants and eight giant tortoises. As we stepped into the house, Michel exclaimed, "*Allahu Akbar*! Allah is Great! We have electricity today!"

***

The smoking Karthala Volcano.

The Comoros comprises, from west to east, the islands of Grande Comore (known as Njazidja), Mohéli (Mwali), Anjouan (Nzwani) and Mayotte (Mahoré). (The names are given in the more commonly known French version and in Comorian Swahili in brackets.) The last remains a French territory (as a so-called 'territorial collectivity') after its voters chose in two referendums (not recognised by the African Union) to stay in France when the rest of the Comoros declared independence in 1995.

The Comorian nation are a mixed people of Arab, African, Malagasy and Creole origins. Arab and French are the official languages. Almost 90% of the population is Sunni Muslim and almost all speak a Comorian dialect of the Swahili language commonly spoken on the east coast of Africa.

This is one of the world's poorest countries, with a GDP per capita of only US$710, and 60% of the population living below the poverty line. Most of its income is derived from agriculture, which employs 80% of the workforce. Yet, it is not self-sufficient in food production: there is limited arable land in the Comoros and political chaos has disrupted cultivation. Besides, its young population is growing too fast at 3% per year, in a country where there are few jobs. Remittances from the 160,000 Comorians living abroad, as well as foreign aid, whether in food or funds, have become a major source of subsistence in this country.

Most notably, the Comoros is the world's largest producer of ylang-ylang, which is used in the production of perfume, and is the world's second largest producer of vanilla. When you have ice cream at Swensen's after shopping for perfume and cologne, think about the Comoros and its *coups d'etat*.

***

We spent our first day here wandering around Moroni. This was a terribly run-down capital. Potholes everywhere, some of which were large enough for one to fall into. It was as though someone had dug three-metre deep holes to lay pipes and then forgot to lay the pipes or cover the holes up. The shops sold substandard merchandise and there were very few restaurants or even simple eating places. We had a brochure with colourful advertisements of hotels and restaurants, but most of them did not seem to operate anymore. Political instability had driven business, tourists and everything good away.

The pathetic state of Moroni also proved the 'Critical Mass Theory' of a Colombian banker friend. According to this theory, a society, no matter how rich or poor, needed to have a certain number of people to support amenities and businesses that made it vibrant, fun and liveable. Once a critical mass in population was achieved, there would always be a sufficiently large middle and upper class to support nice things such as fancy restaurants at reasonable prices, cinemas and bookshops, even though the middle and upper classes may be a small percentage of the population.

Moroni had 24,000 people and the entire island of Grande Comore only 260,000 people. Combined with a GDP per capita of US$710, this was a very small local economy with little spending power. That was why although Madagascar was only slightly better off with a GDP of US$870, its capital of 2 million people (and 16 million in the whole country), Antananarivo, had lots of restaurants, night clubs, cinemas and more.

With a heavy dose of *coup d'etat* fever, it was no wonder few diplomats wanted to be posted here. There were only two foreign embassies here, those of France and China, both of which had political interests to maintain. The Americans had pulled out long ago in 1993.

France, the ex-colonial power, remained Comoros' chief donor. Roads, bridges and construction in many places bore plaques or billboards indicating European Union funding. However, like most mismanaged countries, whatever infrastructure built has been left to deteriorate and eventually fall into disrepair and disuse.

China, faraway from these remote isles, was here for another reason: to ensure that the Comoros did not switch recognition to Taiwan, like Sao Tome and Principe, Nauru, Nicaragua, Paraguay and other poor, small countries. To achieve this, China financed huge infrastructure projects or provided cheap loans to these countries. Taiwan did likewise to those countries that supported her. In the Comoros, China has built a satellite transmission station and a monolith structure called the Palace of Culture, where major state ceremonies and events are held.

When we passed by the Palace of Culture one evening, we heard drums beating and loud music in near absolute darkness. President Azali, who as a colonel in the Army had gained power through a *coup d'etat* in 1999, was attending a major event with local dignitaries in the Palace which was lit up, but since none of the lights outside were working, the cultural dance troupe had to perform in darkness. Even the palace proper itself was in an advanced state of deterioration — some of the window panes were broken and paint was fading from the walls. I was to see a similar lack of maintenance and deterioration of public buildings and infrastructure in Madagascar. Was it the lack of suitable maintenance expertise or funding? One could suppose that the tax revenue has gone to the maintenance of the private villas of these leaders on the French Riviera instead!

***

We discussed if it was worth the effort for corrupt individuals to launch coups in such small and poor countries. My argument was that it probably was, despite the Critical Mass Theory. Take the case of the Comoros, a miserably poor country whose citizens have to work abroad to support their dependents at home. With 160,000 nationals living abroad, they would make expensive international telephone calls — most of the time calling from abroad. Even then, the telecom company would make a fair bit of money and hence a Comoros telecom licence was worth something. If one was a corrupt dictator, that would have been a good cash cow.

Perhaps one decided to build a road, maybe a short one. Aid donors could be approached for US$5 million and then one could get his own construction company involved, or obtain some kickbacks from the company engaged, or even better, steal it directly from the donors, if there were not sufficient controls and monitoring over how funds were disbursed.

***

Apart from massive political upheavals, the country suffered from the eruption of Volcano Karthala in 1977 and cyclones in the 1980s. As the country struggled to rebuild itself in the 1990s, the already

The enchanting dilapidation of old Moroni, capital of the Comoros.

fragmented federation became even smaller when the islands of Anjouan and Moheli declared independence in 1997, leaving only the largest island, Grand Comore, remaining. Anjouan, seeing the prosperity of Mayotte under French rule, asked France to 're-colonise' the island, but received a 'Thanks, but no thanks'. Who would want to support another bankrupt island of little value? In 2002, after failed 'federal' invasions of Anjouan and Moheli, plus mini civil wars and attempted coups in Anjouan, the three islands agreed to reunite again in a loose union known as the Union of Comoros, with substantial autonomy for each of the three island states, which would have their own president and government. So, now there were four presidents (including the federal president) in one tiny country of three islands and 600,000 people!

Just as the new union was set up after four referendums and eight elections, the country was in a state of crisis again. This time, it was the federal president against the president of Grand Comore, where Moroni, the federal capital, was located. Both disagreed on who was to run the army and collect taxes. There we go again, I thought. Would the Islands of the Moon ever be at peace?

***

Michel, the owner of Villa Jessica, was a man of unusual patience. Now in his late 40s, he had spent 37 years on these islands. He was born in Madagascar of French parents, who had then moved to the Comoros. He grew up here and fell in love with the carefree island life. He studied in France and brought his French bride back to these islands.

Since then, he has witnessed 17 attempted *coups d'etat*, which he dismissed as minor gunfights with not more than two or three shots. Some of the coups were staged by white mercenaries who numbered about 20 to 30 men. The moment shots were fired at army barracks and the presidential palace, the 500-strong Comoros Army would surrender immediately. Why risk one's life if one had not been paid for months? The mercenaries and new coup leaders would normally come with promises of full payment of salaries owed by the overthrown government. The new day would begin with soldiers of the Old Army queuing to sign up in the New Army and collecting their promised paychecks.

Whenever a coup occured, Michel would stay at home and give his 'boys' — as he called his Comorian servants — some money to buy meat from the market in order to have home-cooked meals for a few days of self-imposed curfew. One would not want to wander the streets when trigger-happy soldiers were going about looting or searching for supporters of the previous regime.

Michel worked for a French development aid agency but foreign donors were getting tired and impatient. "The Comorians are only interested in fighting among themselves. Every time there is a coup, we are back to square one. The donors feel that they are wasting their money."

Michel also ran a candy factory that used its own generators. He used to run a cookie factory, too, but power shortages had made its operating costs too high. "It's cheaper to import cookies from Madagascar or Tanzania. It's impossible to run production if you get power for 5 hours a day for 2 weeks and then no power for one whole month," he said.

Villa Jessica was his pride and he used to receive a number of tourists. Lately, nobody arrived apart from newly posted French diplomats, aid workers and an occasional adventurous Frenchman living in Mayotte (where there were 10,000 Frenchmen) coming here for a weekend break. Indeed, the only people who were staying there when we arrived were two Frenchmen, an urbane diplomat and an engineer installing the Comoros' first GSM network.

"This is a messed-up country. It's getting worse and worse every year." Michel was frustrated, but one wonders why he has stayed for 37 years. Perhaps he had done so initially in the hope of better days, and thereafter because he no longer had anywhere else to go.

Indeed, he was something of a local notable, or so he claimed: "If you get lost, just tell anyone that you are a friend of Michel Bon Bon and they will bring you here safely." So, remember Michel, the Candy Man.

***

Comoros is one of those places with many versions of its founding story. For a country of this size, there is just too much blood and too many complications, just like its politics.

Here are some of them according to the Library of Congress Area Studies Handbook:

- Local legend cites the first settlement of the archipelago by two families from Arabia after Solomon's death.
- Legend also tells of a Persian King, Husain bin Ali, who established a settlement on Comoros around the beginning of the 11th century. Bantu people apparently moved to Comoros before the 14th century, principally from the coast of what is now southern Mozambique; on the island of Nzwani they apparently encountered an earlier group of inhabitants, a Malayo-Indonesian people.
- A legend is recounted on Comoros and on the East African coast, of seven Shirazi brothers who set sail in seven ships and landed on the coast of northwestern Madagascar and on Njazidja and Nzwani, and established colonies in the 15th century. The Shirazi, who divided Njazidja into 11 sultanates and Nzwani into two, extended their rule to Mahoré and Mwali, although the latter came under the control of Malagasy rulers in the 19th century.

For a small island of 1148km^2 and 11 sultanates, Njazidja (Grand Comore) had way too many sultans! The island needs a major M&A (merger and acquisition) consolidation. Perhaps I should not be too surprised at the separatist tendencies of Anjouan and Moheli, given that there used to be a dozen or more countries on these four islands a century ago.

***

We walked into the National Museum, which was more like a poorly looked-after warehouse of spider-webs, decaying paintings and historic photographs half-eaten by moths. After a principled but ultimately resultless argument with the curator over his attempt to cheat us of some change of insignificant amounts, we aimed for the rare coelacanth exhibits. The coelacanth is a prehistoric family of deep-sea fishes with limb-like fins which man first discovered as fossils. They were thought to have lived 400 million years ago and became extinct 70 million years ago, until live specimens were found in the Comoros in 1938. For a nation with few unique national symbols, the coelacanth has become an icon which appears on souvenirs and public buildings in the Comoros. We found two specimens of the coelacanth: one dusty, dried-up and stuffed specimen hanging from the wall, and another half-decomposed in some dirty-looking fluid in a murky glass container. Were these coelacanths reflective of the state of the nation?

***

A dusty specimen of the Coelacanth, prehistoric fish still found in the Comoros.

In the 16th century, given their strategic location at the entrance of the Mozambique Channel, the Comoros became a prosperous trading centre, but intense competition and warfare between the sultanates — which once in a while recognised an equal amongst them as *sultan tibe* or supreme ruler — led to French intervention and occupation, not unlike that of the white mercenaries in the last quarter of the 20th century.

***

We hired a chauffeured car for one day for 30 euros, excluding fuel, to bring us on a round-island drive. We drove along the coast, passing many fishing villages, assorted baobab trees and many fading, over-hyped EU-sponsored billboards proclaiming yet another anonymous-looking hamlet as a 'National Historic & Natural Site', when there was nothing more than a few coconut trees and the local rubbish dump. The streets of Comoros' rural towns and villages were full of activity — yes, of men sitting around chatting and smoking, and children running around, shouting and screaming.

Only the women — if they were not fully hidden in black *burqas*, their faces would be thickly covered with a layer of yellow ash that they said would enrich their skin and make them look prettier — were working in the way that we recognise it as such in the outside world: washing of clothing, selling vegetables and looking after children. Who needed to work in the Comoros? One would usually just wait for one's son's monthly remittances from Paris. Nobody needed to plough the fields anymore. Just wait for the next food parcel from concerned American churches. Aid has destroyed the work ethic in many African countries.

The only promise lay in the Comoros Vanilla Plant in Mbeni on the northeastern coast of Grande Comore. This was one of the only two vanilla and ylang ylang refining facilities still operating in the Comoros. Years of chaos and neglect have led to the closure of all the other plants. Nowadays, the raw materials are shipped instead to peaceful and serene Mayotte, which exported more refined ylang ylang than the Comoros. This smallish plant also experimented with other farm products, local handicraft and the rearing of ostriches. I had pressing questions about economies of scale and the lack of focus on core businesses, but have to salute these brave young men and women who operate in such adverse circumstances. As a token of appreciation, we bought some ylang ylang extracts and local crafts. I wished them success. Even in the seemingly hopeless Comoros, there was some hope.

***

On 3 August 1975, i.e. 28 days after independence was declared, President Abdallah was overthrown by a crazy unscrupulous character named Ali Soilih, with the assistance of foreign mercenaries. Soilih then began his programme to turn the Comoros into a Red Revolutionary bastion. He started his own version of China's Red Guards a la the Cultural Revolution. He wanted to abolish the wearing of veils and the traditional practice of grand marriage, thus provoking the wrath of the nation. However, ironically, it was not the people of the Comoros who overthrew him. In 1977, Soilih's

The friendly people of the Comoros.

predecessor, Abdallah, was returned to power after a coup by the same white mercenaries who overthrew him in 1975. Soilih was mysteriously killed days after the coup.

The real power behind the throne was now Bob Denard, the legendary French mercenary chieftain, who was involved in a range of coups, civil wars, revolutions, counter-revolutions and other serious mischief worldwide, from Vietnam to Biafra. Together with the puppet President Abdallah, he (officially the Chief of the Presidential Guards) made the Comoros the base of his new dodgy business empire that controlled 70% of the national economy and cosied up to the apartheid regime of South Africa, which made use of the Comoros to bust international sanctions and supply arms to rebels in Mozambique.

A series of mysterious events then occurred in 1989, which resulted in yet another slaying of a Comorian President. It was said that Abdallah was shot by Denard after disagreement over business matters, and Denard seized power from the provisional president in yet another coup. Another puppet president was imposed: the Comoros' third president in less than a week. This sparked off a popular uprising against the mercenaries. Denard fled to South Africa but returned in 1995 to stage yet another coup. This time, France intervened by sending in its forces. Denard was arrested, put on trial in Paris for the murder of President Abdallah (of which he was acquitted), and so ended his exploits once and for all. Of course, he went on to write his autobiography.

***

We drove past the Galawa Beach, which once played host to a Sun International luxury resort hotel that has since closed down. This beach has an unusual connection with a Comorian member of the Al Qaeda network named Fazul. In 1996, he masterminded the hijack of an Ethiopian Airlines plane which crashed on this beach. Seventy-nine of the 127 passengers died, including seven key Israeli defence and aerospace industries executives, the head of CIA's Horn of Africa operations and the head of the Ukrainian military intelligence. Fazul then went into hiding as a poor Moroni fisherman, only to resurface again in 1998, when he, as Commander of the East African Al Qaeda forces, executed the bombing of the US embassies in Kenya and Tanzania. He then went into hiding again.

Coconut trees swayed in the background as we sped past. All was quiet on the southern front.

***

Three days were enough for Grande Comore. We had seen what we had wanted to see. It was out of the question to visit the crater of the Karthala (which used to be a major attraction for adventure travellers) whose seismic activity had continued to increase. It was time to depart for Mayotte, the island that rejected independence in a politically-incorrect decision that scandalised nationalists and leftists everywhere, and yet it was so wise a decision in hindsight. For the three independent islands of the Comoros, freedom has been a mere illusion, a state that existed in name but not in substance.

"Bon voyage!" Michel waved farewell to us as we left for the airport. "Maybe in a few days' time, the volcano will erupt and this whole island, including myself, will be at the bottom of the Indian Ocean."

I watched Michel's oversized silhouette shrinking to nothingness as our car sped northwards to the airport. Where would this man be in five years' time? I am sure he would still be here in Moroni. Every land needs a great survivor like him.

Postscript:

The Union of Comoros still survives. In 2006, the country saw its first ever peaceful handing over of power to a new president who defeated a candidate supported by the incumbent in an election. In 2008, the African

Union launched an invasion on the island of Anjouan to defeat its separatist president who rigged the local elections and wanted to break away from Comoros. The Union seems safe, for the moment.

Mayotte and Réunion — A Rendezvous with France in Africa (2003)

Some say that the sun has set on empires after Hong Kong became Chinese territory in 1997. This description may well be wrong, as old empires like the British and the French still exist in remnants, albeit in the forms of small islands scattered across oceans and continents. (Of course, those more sceptical amongst us would talk about the new American empire and its unincorporated territories and new and old satellite states, or of the Chinese state in the vast non-Han territories in the West.) I have always loved visiting political oddities, imperial remnants or not, and it was with this in mind that I visited French outposts in the Indian Ocean, Mayotte and Réunion, each of which has its own unique history and political status.

The French once ruled huge tracts of Africa. Today, the continent is mostly independent, if you ignore the sizeable French economic and military presence in many of its ex-colonies, where it continues to pull strings, either through legal aid, under-table money, or occasional military intervention. Indeed, a former French foreign minister once said that Africa was the only continent where France could still "change the course of history with a few hundred men".

It is in Mayotte and Réunion that France continues to rule, officially. Colonies are politically incorrect these days and hence the great powers use fanciful names for them. France has various categories of DOM-TOMs (*Départements d'Outre-Mer* & *Territoires d'Outre-Mer*). Guadeloupe, Martinique and French Guiana in the Caribbean, and

Réunion are DOMs, or Overseas Departments of France. This means they are treated as part of France, not mere colonies. New Caledonia, Wallis and Futuna and French Polynesia are TOMs, or Overseas Territories, perhaps a nicer word for colonies. Between the extremes of DOM and TOM is a category known as *Collectivité Territoriale* (Territorial Collectivity), which is like a form of semi-departmental status. Mayotte and St. Pierre & Miquelon (a small group of islands near Canada) belong to this category.

***

We arrived on an Air Austral flight from Moroni, with a spectacular view of the rebel islands of Anjouan and Mohéli along the way. Before that, we had to identify our luggage on the runway as Mayotte-bound before boarding the plane — that was probably necessary in an airport without automated baggage tracking or loading. One felt safer that way, too.

The French tricolour fluttered in the terminal building and the bored but friendly French gendarmerie stamped my passport. No frills, no hassle from taxi drivers, no loud outpour of emotions. Just plain, simple business-like reception in a clean proper airport terminal building. The Euro is in use here, not the dodgy colourful banknotes of the Comoros Franc. A tourist information office was located just outside the terminal, where we picked up some maps and brochures. In the Comoros, the tourism department had long closed its doors. We hopped into a taxi. Seventy cents would bring us to the jetty where we were to take a ferry to Mamoudzou, the capital of Mayotte on the main island of Grande Terre.

There, we would find supermarkets, post offices, bookshops, ATM/ cash machines, restaurants and hotels. We were back to a normal country.

***

At 374 sq km in area, Mayotte is the eastern-most island of the Comoros chain. It is a mountainous island with volcanic peaks and surrounded by a barrier reef 200km long, encircling a lagoon with a surface area of 1,500km^2 — one of the world's largest.

The Mahorais (or people of Mayotte) have always maintained that they were not really Comorians. The island's original Comorian inhabitants were either massacred or enslaved by raiders from the Sakalava tribes of nearby Madagascar. When the Merina tribe of the Madagascar highlands conquered the Sakalava kingdoms, some members of this tribe fled to Mayotte, where they inter-married with the remaining original Mahorais as well as visiting Swahili and Arab traders, thus forming the Mahorais people of today.

Mayotte was the first of the Comoro Islands to fall under French rule. In 1841, the local Malagasy sultan ceded the island to France in exchange for cash and French education for his children. The other islands were taken by France much later, in 1886. Thus, the Mahorais claim that they are more European and culturally different from the Comorians. The desire to be French, or at least non-Comorian, has therefore always been strong here.

Dzaoudzi, a town in Mayotte, was in fact the capital of French Comoros from 1841 to 1962, when the seat of the colonial government was moved to Moroni on Grande Comore. By the 1970s, when the issue of independence for the Comoros had been negotiated, the

The dock side market of Mayotte's capital, Mamoudzou.

critical question was whether the referendum for independence should have been considered for the entire island chain as a whole, or island by island, which was what dissenting politicians from Mayotte wanted.

In December 1974, a referendum was held, as a result of which 95% of the voters of the three western islands of the Comoros voted for independence, but in Mayotte, 65% voted against independence. The Mahorais had long felt that they were a different people from the Comorians and many were suspicious of the government in Moroni, which they saw as corrupt and would almost certainly neglect the interests of Mayotte. The Mahorais leaders called for a second referendum in late 1976 to prove that the Mahorais wanted to 'remain French to be free' (*nous resterons franáais pour rester libre*). This was supported by the French parliament, which passed an Act postponing independence for six months and with a second referendum to follow.

Infuriated, the Comoros government in Moroni declared independence of the entire chain of islands from France unilaterally on 6 July 1975. The French reacted by cutting all aid and sending its navy to defend Mayotte from any invasion from the new Comoros state, which soon received UN recognition in its entirety, including the French-controlled island of Mayotte. The Comoros' claim over Mayotte was also recognised by the African Union.

Given Mayotte's unusual status (i.e. international recognition of the Comoros' claim) which was an embarrassment for the French, a special status of *collectivité territoriale* was created as a temporary solution. Perhaps the French thought that they might persuade the Mahorais to rejoin the Comoros in due course.

Of course, with every year that passes, that aim has increasingly become less of a possibility. As the Comoros slide into the abyss of revolution, counter-revolution, economic crisis and chaos, the people of Mayotte continue to enjoy a guaranteed monthly minimum wage of US$400, French citizenship, peace and economic prosperity.

For the Mahorais, the goal now, as proclaimed in the brochure published by the local government, is to become a full French overseas department by 2008.

The leaders of Mayotte in that fateful year of 1975 must have been denounced as traitors and colonial running dogs by the Comorians, as well as the leaders of Africa and the Third World at that time. The Mahorais today must have been very thankful for the decision of their leaders. That decision might have been against the mainstream ideological belief at that time, but it has saved Mayotte from the sad fate of the Comoros.

***

We did not do much in Mayotte. We stayed in a simple, pleasant homestay run by a friendly elderly French lady who spoke no English. It was spartan in comparison to Villa Jessica in Moroni, but then, in easy-to-do and as-safe-as-you-get Mayotte, where the tourist office was always around the corner to assist, one did not need much. Tap water was drinkable and everything one could have wanted was available at the supermarket. That was perfect except for the prices, which were in euros and everything was quite expensive, given that most things were imported. The vast harbour and the lagoon were full of yachts and other pleasure crafts. Peace and prosperity had encouraged tourists and pleasure-seekers. It was time to relax, after the stress and hassle of the Comoros. Perhaps I had become soft, after the comforts of Mauritius and the Seychelles.

Mayotte was culturally similar to the Comoros. We walked around the local fresh produce market where many women were dressed in robes with a distinctive red-white floral pattern which immediately reminded us that this was still part of the Comoros cultural sphere.

After many years of peace, Mayotte had become an abode for the poor and persecuted of the region. Many Comorians try to get into Mayotte, to work there for higher wages, or to use it as a springboard to France. In 1975, after ethnic riots against Comorians broke out in Majunga in northern Madagascar, many Madagascar Comorians fled here. We met a taxi driver who was once a victim of that ethnic cleansing. He had fled here with his family after the riots and had ended up driving a taxi around Mayotte.

We did not stay very long in Mayotte and flew to the island of Réunion.

***

La Réunion, meaning 'The Meeting' in French, must be the place with the most boring, understated name in the world. The island, located 800km east of Madagascar and 220km west of Mauritius, was first named after the Bourbon Dynasty of France. However, after the French Revolution, it was renamed Réunion after the Colonial Assembly itself. It was as though the city of Washington DC had been renamed The Congress. The revolutionaries in charge of Réunion must not have been imaginative people.

In some ways, Réunion resembles Mauritius. Both are French-speaking and have their own version of the Creole tongue, although it is said that the Réunionnais version is supposed to be more difficult to understand than the Mauritian one for French speakers, although

Réunion is part of France. Both have the same racial groups: Creole (descendants of African slaves), Indians, Chinese and Europeans. The cuisines of both islands are a delightful fusion of French seafood cuisine mixed with mild Indian curries and hints of Chinese and Malagasy influences. In Réunion, the Creoles are the largest group at 40% of the population, whereas the Indians dominate Mauritius at 50%. The Chinese account for 3% of the population on both islands. Over 30% of the Réunionnais are Europeans, whereas they comprise only 3% of the Mauritian population.

Whilst Mauritius is an independent country, Réunion is a French overseas department, i.e. it is an integral part of France instead of being a colony, although located far, far away from mainland France ('La Métropole'). This has a significant impact on the island's development and the way it is run.

The Réunionnais are French citizens and enjoy the same minimum wages and social security system as those in France. In fact, civil servants are paid the same wages. The net result of this is the 40% unemployment rate. Given the island's isolated geographical location and the labour force's productivity and skills set which is less than that of a developed country, unrealistically high wage levels discourage investment and industrial development. With such a high unemployment rate, the burden on the French social security system is heavy. More than 10% of France's social security spending is spent in DOM-TOMs like Réunion, whose total population is less than 1% of France. French taxpayers are increasingly aware of such policy failures and it is a matter of time before reforms will be taken to reduce that drain. I wonder about the impact of such changes: a decline in the local economy, or perhaps even calls for independence? Government aspirations per se cannot change economics.

French subsidy of the remote department has a more visible impact — incredibly good motorways which bring one from the capital, St. Denis in the north, to St. Pierre 100km to the south, in less than one and a half hours. The bus network uses impressive new coaches and public amenities are clean, modern and well maintained. Even the airport terminal building at St. Denis is the typical huge glass-and-steel complex that one sees in major international airports, in contrast to the often provincial looking ones I had seen elsewhere on this journey.

***

We had a late dinner at a Chinese restaurant in St. Denis shortly after arrival. We did not fancy reading the French menu and so asked if there was a chef Chinois. A smiling Chinese chef in his late 30s came out and welcomed us in Cantonese. He was originally from Hong Kong and had been there for 18 years (he must have been there since his teens). He was happy to see us and spoke to us in Cantonese. We had wonderful hot and sour soup, a great relief in the cold weather.

***

If someone were to punch his fist into an almost flat rugby ball, he would get a ball with the same contour as Réunion. The island rises up gently from the depths of the Indian Ocean, and then suddenly

The bizarre mix of Alpine and tropical landscapes in Cilaos, Reunion.

soars up steeply heading for the heavens like the tall brown walls of a forbidden fortress. As sudden as it is, the contour falls off into an abyss, and below are green inland basins — soft, cosy and delicious like the flesh of the durian fruit concealed within thick treacherous thorns. Millions of years ago, volcanic eruptions in Réunion blew up parts of the central volcanic highlands of the island, creating huge natural amphitheatres more than 10km wide, with dramatic cliff sides amidst Alpine peaks. The tallest peak here, Piton des Neiges, is 3,069m, and the active volcano further south, Piton de la Fournaise, is 2,510m. The green basins between these peaks are known as *Cirques*, or circus, and they are the little Switzerlands of this volcanic isle.

We took an early bus across this island of 2,510km^2, from St. Denis to St. Louis in the south, where we switched to another bus for Cilaos in the mountains. We drove initially along the green coastal plains, where the modern housing estates, quaint farmhouses and casual footpaths along the sandy beaches reminded us more of the coast of Bordeaux than that of Africa. As we headed inland for the Cirque de Cilaos, rose gardens gave way to sugar cane plantations, which in turn gave way to pine as the road started to twist and wind, like a snake uncertain of its way. The road climbed into the mountains, scaling the cliffs and treacherous pathways. A few careless swings of the steering wheel would bring one into the canyon below. Around us were sharp vertical cliffs and grey Alpine peaks hardened by million of years of clashes of intercontinental volcanic plates, all of which look a thousand miles away from the soft, pleasant suburbia we had just left behind.

This forbidding road was once the escape route of slaves working in the plantations on the plains. Called the Marrons, they fled deep inland to these hidden valleys, where they set up independent republics of free men until the slave-owners and bounty hunters caught up with them, hunted them down and demonstrated that it did not pay to be free. Today, all that remains of that dark era are the rocks, caves and valleys which are named after the more famous of those who fought bravely but in vain.

Suddenly, we found that the canyon opened up to a concealed

inner basin of greenery and small farmsteads. We had arrived in Cilaos, the largest settlement of the Cirques of the same name. Here, Alpine chalets, church towers, small lakes and misty mountains almost convinced us that we were in the Alps rather than the Indian Ocean.

We stayed at a nice hotel which once played host to colonial officers recovering from the fevers of Cambodia and the toils of fighting the southern tribes of Madagascar. We strolled around the beautiful gardens and lakes of this small town, once a timeless farming community-turned-spa resort, now an escape from the more hectic St. Denis and the coast. We walked a short trail and tried the local rum and wine; the latter tasted more like vinegar and the combination gave me a bad headache, which offset the pleasant effects of this earthly paradise.

***

Two nights in Réunion and off we flew to Antananarivo, capital of the world's fourth largest island and a mad, mad place!

POSTSCRIPT:

In 2009, Mayotte voted overwhelmingly to become an overseas department of France, i.e. to be part of France proper, with full application of French laws and most attractively, of French welfare and healthcare systems.

Madagascar — Erotic Tombs, Tribal Warriors and Bull Fights in the Great Red Island (2003)

Madagascar, the world's fourth largest island at over 1,600km long and 570km wide, is also known as the Great Red Island due to its red soil. Due to serious deforestation and tavy, which is slash and burn farming, Madagascar's red soil is increasingly being exposed and eroded. The red soil is washed into the rivers, which stain them blood red and this, in turn, is carried to the ocean. An aerial view, when flying over the island, reveals how red the whole place is. Madagascar gives a whole new meaning to the expression 'environmental degradation'.

Madagascar is a land with unique fauna and flora, a result of its isolation. This land was once part of the great island Gondwana, which included Africa, India, Australia and South America 250 million years ago. As Gondwana split apart due to volcanic activity and continental drifts, the various continents were formed and Madagascar came into being as it split off into a separate land mass 65 million years ago.

As a result of its isolation and the late arrival of mankind to the island only 2,000 years ago, Madagascar's wildlife has been able to evolve independently from those of other continents and, hence, acquired characteristics which are unique. This is what makes this island special in the eyes of scientists and animal lovers. However, as we were to discover later, the unique natural heritage of Madagascar is rapidly disappearing, as its human population continues to grow and uncontrolled and unplanned agricultural activity destroys the island's surface cover.

I am pessimistic about the protection of Madagascar's wildlife. If I ever return to this land in the future, I would not be surprised if most of the wildlife which I had seen on this trip would be found only in zoos and nowhere else.

***

We arrived in the evening at the airport of the capital, Antananarivo — a mouthful of a name! Something which we discovered in Madagascar was that pronouncing Malagasy names could be a tongue-twisting exercise. For example, try saying the name of one of the country's greatest kings — Andrianampoinimerina — and even that is the short form for Andrianampoinimerinandriantsimitoviaminandriampanjaka. Fortunately, the capital had a shorter alternative, Tana.

Malagasy bureaucrats are world renowned for their 'super-efficiency' that even the Swiss take their hats off to. Given that there was only one flight arriving that evening, the fact that it took us more than an hour and a half to clear Malagasy passport control was testimony to their 'efficiency'. All foreigners required visas to enter and everyone had to queue up to pay for the visa stamps. Next was the queue to get the passports checked. Each visitor had the honour of having his passport checked by at least four officers, each of whom had to sign and counter sign the passport and other slips of paper floating around the passport control box — what a perfectionist system of internal control to ensure checks and counter-checks to prevent corruption and infiltration of international terrorists. Madagascar was certainly doing its part in the War Against Terrorism!

Once we cleared passport control and customs check — we saw Malagasy people being examined with their luggage opened but, fortunately, foreigners were spared — we were set upon by 30 people offering us taxi transfers, money exchange, porter services and god-knows-what services. What sweet people, each shouting and screaming at the top of their voices and some grabbing our luggage and threatening to tear our limbs apart.

"Hang on, hands off, HANDS OFF!"

We had to shout to prevent ourselves from been torn to pieces. "We have people picking us up!"

That dissuaded the taxi drivers, but others continued to hassle us.

"Get away! Get away!" I asked around for the people from Hotel Sakamanga, who had agreed via email to pick us up, while E proceeded to change some euros into Malagasy francs, though not before fighting off some black marketeers.

After the money had been changed, there was still no sign of the Sakamanga folks, so I negotiated with a man to drive us to town for FMG50,000 (about US$7). Fine, but I found six people following us to the car, some symbolically giving us a hand by holding on to a strap or two of my backpack. As we placed our luggage into the rundown car (which would have successfully made it to the scrapyard if it was in Singapore), a few of them asked for money for having 'helped' us with the luggage.

"No way, no way. We carried our own stuff — none of you helped us!" What a ridiculous demand! "Go away!"

Meanwhile, E was arguing with another man who insisted that E should change money with him. When E said that he had already changed his money, that man said that E was lying because he could not have done so in such a short time.

"Let's go! Let's go," I told the driver, as four or five pairs of hands were still holding onto the car door, with their ridiculous demands for money. So off we went.

Fifty metres down the road, I shouted to the driver, "Can we stop now? I need to check our luggage in the boot." I was worried about the mass of people around the car and wondered if our luggage was still intact. I got out of the car and checked that everything was okay.

At this point, a man walked over and waved a card which looked like some form of a licence and said, "I'm the official airport taxi. You are not allowed to take illegal transport."

Our driver shouted, "Get in the car! Quick!" I jumped into the car, slammed the car door shut and the driver sped away as fast as he could into the dark, unlit roads. At that point, I asked myself where on earth we were heading off to; if he decided to rob and kill us, there was nothing we could do.

Forty minutes later, we found ourselves at Hotel Sakamanga.

"Welcome to Madagascar!"

***

The origins of the Malagasy people is a mystery for historians and anthropologists. Anthropological and linguistic evidence suggests that the Malagasy people were the descendants of mariners from Indonesia who came here 1,500 to 2,000 years ago, and these immigrants mixed with the Bantu people who moved over from Africa across the Mozambique Channel. Linguists place the Malagasy language within

Eternal Africa.

Lobster seller at a local market.

the Malay-Polynesian family of languages and believe that it is closest to a tribal language in Borneo, although no one knows how or why they would have sailed so far across the Indian Ocean to Madagascar. Indeed, when we listened to Malagasy music, we found that it sounded amazingly similar to the Malay or Indonesian languages, although it is more difficult to find any perfect match of words. The facial features of the Malagasy people, especially those living in the Highlands, also resemble those of Indonesians. Walking around Tana, we often thought we were in Downtown Jakarta. In addition, the Malagasy also eat rice as a staple like the Indonesians, unlike their African neighbours who tend to eat cassava and other tuber roots. In fact, the Malagasy eat more rice per capita than any other nation in the world.

***

Tana, capital of Madagascar. The city was founded in 1610 by King Adrianjaka of the Merina people, the most Indonesian-looking of the 18 Malagasy tribes. He placed a garrison of a thousand men here and called the city Antananarivo, meaning 'Town of the Thousand'. On top of a hill, he built a Rova or palace. The capital was moved here by King Andrianampoinimerina at the end of the 18th century from Ambohimanga, 20km to the north. From here, his son and successor, King Radama I, went on to conquer all of Madagascar so that his kingdom would have no frontier but the sea. The French came and they, too, ruled the colony from the city, which was located near the geographical centre of the island.

The impressive European-style Rova, also known as the Queen's Palace on account of most of Madagascar's 19th century monarchs having been female, sits on the top of a hill — one of the 12 upon which the city was built — overlooking the city and pretty Lake Anosy. This used to be the heart of the old Kingdom of Madagascar, the focal point of attention of the nation and its capital. Queen Ranavalona I was renowned for dropping her less-favoured subjects off the cliffs from here.

The Rova was also the resting place of the monarchs whose tombs were venerated for good harvest and fortune.

On 6 November 1995, an arsonist burned down the entire Rova, including the royal tombs in an attack that destroyed one of the most important treasures and historical heritage of the Malagasy people and nation. Eighty percent of the historical artefacts, antiques and historical documents within the complex were destroyed. For the people of Madagascar, for whom ancestral worship and veneration of the remains of the dead are important, the destruction of the royal tombs was spiritual as well. The soul of the nation was burned to ashes. Today, only the facades of the Rova remain. A slow process of reconstruction is continuing and a museum nearby displays the artefacts which had been rescued.

We visited the ruins of the Rova and the museum. There were a number of old photos of Malagasy royalty in Western court dress, as well as an exchange of letters with Queen Victoria of the British Empire, with whom the Malagasy monarchy maintained close contact until the invasion and abolition of the Malagasy state by the French in 1896.

Like Thailand and Ethiopia, Madagascar woke up to the reality of European expansion in the 19th century. Malagasy monarchs realised that without modernisation and international diplomacy, the nation would soon be doomed like many of its neighbours in Africa. It acquired the trappings of a modern state, such as the adaptation of Western court attire and protocol, the building of Western style palaces, the setting up of modern administrative structures and the modernisation of the army.

Like Thailand and Ethiopia, Malagasy monarchs faced enormous internal opposition towards reforms. However, in the case of Madagascar, its monarchs were not powerful enough to overcome conservative opposition and a few kings and queens were assassinated by their enemies. Through a mixture of domestic reforms and international diplomacy, Thailand and Ethiopia were able to remain independent. Madagascar, however, eventually succumbed to international intrigue.

By the 1890s, the British, who had enormous interest in Madagascar, agreed to trade Madagascar for Zanzibar, thus allowing the French to march in and abolish the monarchy in 1896, with the last queen, Ranvalona III, exiled to Algeria.

The Rova today is nothing but a ghost of its past. The Malagasy nation does not seem to have recovered from its decline. The great blow was dealt when the arsonist's torch destroyed the last remnants of its royal past. The cold winter winds howl as though the ghosts of the dead monarchs are crying over the loss of the palace and the state of the nation. The Malagasy flag flutters with a mix of bright red, white and green.

***

In the mid-1980s, Chinese martial arts or Kungfu became very popular in Madagascar and Kungfu associations soon developed into paramilitary groups in a bizarre episode of Malagasy history. In late 1984, President Ratsiraka banned the practise of Kungfu as Kungfu associations emerged as rival centres of power. In December 1984, clashes broke out between Kungfu associations and the presidential guards. Clashes continued until July 1986, when army units backed by armoured cars and helicopters finally destroyed the headquarters of the Kungfu groups, killing its leader and 200 followers, thus ending the Kungfu threat to the state once and for all.

***

Tana is now a city of 2 million people. Its streets are dirty, narrow and crowded with vehicles, not to mention the numerous hawkers selling newspapers, batteries, snacks and goodness-knows-what-else to those caught in traffic. It is chaotic, unplanned and simply bloody messy. The streets look as though they have never been widened since the French left in 1960. Two to three storey buildings share downtown city blocks with rice paddy fields and vegetable gardens.

The exodus of the rural landless to the city has enlarged the city far beyond what its original planners had intended — a typical Third World disaster scenario.

Madagascar is a terribly mismanaged country. Since its independence in 1960, the country has gone through coups, uprising and general chaos, not to mention nearly two decades of gross misrule by a former admiral who first destroyed the economy by turning to socialism — President Ratsiraka even wrote his own little red book — and then dramatically turned the country to capitalism, i.e. the crony and corrupt kind that excluded real free markets, accountability and checks and balances.

Madagascar is the seventh poorest country in the world. In a survey of 175 countries, Madagascar ranks 149th in the human development index. Life expectancy is only 53 and only 35% of the population has completed primary education. We witnessed extreme poverty everywhere, although we saw relatively little begging compared to other developing countries. There were, however, many street children and homeless people. We walked past a market one evening and suddenly realised that what we thought were plastic bags of rubbish on the ground were actually homeless people sleeping under multiple layers of rags and plastic sheets. This was at the height of winter and it was freezing cold to live in such conditions. It was bad enough to be poor, but it was certainly worse being poor in a cold country.

In addition, Madagascar has the dubious reputation of being the third most corrupt country in the world after Bangladesh and Nigeria, sharing its ranking with Paraguay and Angola. Many times during our journey, the drivers we engaged were asked for bribes by corrupt police officers at numerous checkpoints. Even as we departed the country at Tana airport, various uniformed officers were asking for money with a casualness that emphasised how ingrained corruption was in this country.

It is no wonder that a BBC correspondent once wrote: "Madagascar is a land of tremendous potential. It always will be. There's an inertia here, with logistical and economic problems that make it almost impossible to see anyone taking over control."

***

We flew south to Toliara, the provincial capital in the poorest and least inhabited part of the country. This area was a dry semi-desert of spiny forests and low shrubs on the southern coast of Madagascar. The tribes of this region, the Vezo and Mahafaly, are among the most 'African' of the Malagasy tribes. Tall and shining dark in complexion, they hardly display any of the Asian features common among the Merina people of the Highlands around Tana.

The Mahafaly are also famous for their impressive tombs. These

The elaborate tombs of the Mahafaly people in the south of Madagascar, with motifs relating to everyday life, mythology, dreams and other earthly pursuits.

tombs tend to be mini buildings painted with bright colours, featuring scenes from the lives of those buried within. We saw themes ranging from traditional ones such as zebu fights — zebus are the omnipresent Malagasy bulls with a distinctive hump on their backs — and country life, to contemporary ones featuring space shuttles and aircrafts, including one with Leonardo di Caprio and Kate Winslet together, with the inscription 'Titanic'. Many tombs also had zebu horns on them symbolising power, and some had stelae and poles with elaborate carvings, including some which were erotic in nature. All this contrasted deeply with the state of abject poverty in this region, where many lived in huts made of leaves and tree branches, the only mitigating factor being the region's temperature, which was mostly hot during the day, but would drop drastically in the evenings. I wondered whether the after-life was considered to be more important than the present.

The Malagasy people are famous for their veneration of the dead. The Highland tribes practise a ceremony known as *famadihana*, the turning of the bones, which is an occasion for rejoicing rather than mourning. Periodically, the dead are exhumed, washed and rewrapped in new shrouds. Relatives visit the dead, and celebrate their lives with pomp and ceremony, and drinking and feasting, after which the dead are returned to their graves accompanied with many gifts.

This was also lobster country. We saw the largest lobsters in the local market, bought some for a song and got someone to cook them for us. The pleasures of life!

***

Madagascar is a big country with awful roads and poor public transport. Route Nationale 7 (RN7), which stretches from Tana (in the middle of the country) to the south disappears into mud and sand in some areas. The most common form of public transport is the *taxi-brousse*, or bush taxi, which can be any type of vehicle, usually with luggage tied to the top, and human capacity squeezed to the maximum, together with assorted chickens, ducks and furniture that accompany the passengers. Our original plan was to take the *taxi-brousse* from south to north, but given that they take a long time to reach any destination and that they do not depart on regular hours, we had to seek more costly alternatives to travel RN7 in the short timescale that we had.

Therefore, whilst in Tana, we arranged for a chauffeured car to bring us from Toliara back to Tana over a period of eight days, stopping at various cities and national parks along the way. Tobi, the designated driver, was unable to make it in time and so a taxi was arranged to pick us up in Toliara and drive us through to Isalo National Park, where Tobi waited for us.

We went off northwards along RN7. It was a dry, dry road, passing through miserably poor hamlets with surprisingly cheerful people. Despite their poverty, we found the Malagasy people most hospitable and friendly. They also loved to be photographed. Everywhere, the locals urged us to take their photos and no payment was ever asked. This had to be paradise for those who loved taking portrait shots in exotic locations.

We also passed a few baobab trees. The baobab is a magnificent

Magnificent baobab trees in southern Madagascar.

tree with a straight, thick bulging stem, quite often with branches concentrated at the very top. In Madagascar, where rainfall is scarcer than in continental Africa, baobab branches sometimes look disproportionately small compared to their tall thick trunk. In Africa, the baobab tree exerts an aura that is legendary. The baobab is large and often lives for a long time, as it is often too large to be chopped down. As such, they are often meeting places and local landmarks, not only for humans but animals as well. Their trunks store water and provide clean drinking relief for travellers in the desert. Village elders tell tales beside them and animals rest under them. They are the source of goodness and wisdom in African folklore, and are surreal and photogenic for the traveller.

Before we reached Isalo National Park, we passed two sapphire towns, Sakaraha and Ilakaka. This was the local equivalent of the Wild West, with settlements that sprouted up overnight with the discovery of sapphires. For a region renowned for its poverty, there were islands of bustling shops, restaurants, bars, casinos, inns and vices of every kind — women in bright dresses and overly heavy makeup seemed to be in great supply here compared to Toliara. We did not stay for long in these dodgy places as we stuck out like sore thumbs. Drunken miners and working girls stared at us, while the police subjected our taxi drivers to long chats (and bribe demands) at every checkpoint along that stretch of RN7.

Many people thought we were Thai, as many of them come here to buy sapphires. They have even set up their own hotel for collective security and familiarity, complete with neon lights and a sign that proclaimed 'Casino'. We saw a smartly dressed Thai trader in his chauffeured car at a police checkpoint. He passed a thick bundle of banknotes to the police and drove past the checkpoint in no time, whereas we spent many minutes with the officer as he examined our documents and extracted a few extra francs from our driver.

***

At Isalo, we met our driver Tobi, a nice 40-plus man who knew what the travellers wanted. He had a pair of sharp eyes and was able to spot village celebrations and feasts two hundred metres away. He would drive up muddy tracks so that travellers were given an exotic visual and emotional feast of Madagascar's colourful village life and culture. He is the man I would recommend for any journey through the Great Red Island. Those who know how thrifty I am would be pleased to know that I tipped him well, to the tune of a decent proportion of the country's per capita GDP.

We also met Rainer, a cheerful German finance controller who squeezed in a Malagasy cycling trip between work in South Africa and a business trip to China. We had many discussions on the world of adventure travel, business and finance. We did a few treks together in the national park, the Malagasy answer to the Grand Canyon, and punctuated our complaints of mud and deforestation with discussions about the troubles of the global auto industry and effective hedging strategies.

Madagascar is renowned for its wildlife, not so much for its abundance, but rather, its uniqueness and the fact that its many rare endemic species are under unprecedented threat from deforestation and human population growth. The lemur is Madagascar's chief mascot and poster boy. It is a cute, monkey-like creature, often with a long tail and rather slow reflexes. They are the ancestors of all apes, including man, and the missing link in the chain of evolution. Their slowness and sleepiness rendered them uncompetitive in the food chain and hence they had long disappeared from the African mainland and elsewhere. In Madagascar, however, in the absence of other primates (such as monkeys), large predators and, until 2,000 years ago, humans, the lemurs have survived and evolved separately. The lemurs are now under threat, the giant lemur and other species having disappeared a long time ago. Fourteen species remain and these cute creatures have lured many tourists to this country, in the hope of seeing them before they disappear for good.

We walked around the national park in search of lemurs. We had been warned that deforestation and poaching had become so serious that tourists often have to go to the zoo in Tana at the end of their trip to see lemurs. We were lucky: we saw three species at Isalo and would also see a few more species in other national parks during the rest of our journey.

***

We sped eastwards, heading for the Highlands. We entered the country of the Bara, a fierce warrior tribe who valued their zebus more highly than anything else. Tradition had it that every young Bara had to prove his manhood by stealing a few zebus, and only then could he prove his worth among the Bara girls. The zebu symbolises wealth and power to the Malagasy people, and this was even more so in the case of the Bara. All major ceremonies were accompanied by the sacrifice of zebus. That was why the Bara guarded their zebus with their lives.

A Bara warrior with his rifle, and a bright red China-made 'double happiness' woolen blanket.

Bad roads!

We passed a few zebu herds with their masters on these dry savannah plains. We stopped by a young fierce-looking warrior armed with an ancient rifle and a red Chinese woollen blanket wrapped tightly around his torso — they used to be dressed in zebu skin but the Chinese factory-manufactured alternative was cheaper and better in fighting the cold. We asked one how many zebus he owned. "Three hundred," said the proud warrior with a faint smile, and asked for some cookies as a present.

The climate became colder when we moved into the Highlands. We spent a night in the city of Fianarantsoa, the 'Place Where Good Is Learned' as it is known in Malagasy, also the intellectual and academic centre of Madagascar. Despite its reputation, the city was a dump and a disappointment, and the rain made everything worse. It was crowded and dilapidated, and we could hardly find any cheap Internet place.

The only respite was the Panda Restaurant, the best Chinese restaurant we found in this corner of the Indian Ocean. It was run by a Chinese man in his mid-30s with a surprisingly Bohemian ponytail. The wonton soup was fantastic, and the wonton tender and well-wrapped. There were over 20,000 Chinese people in Madagascar and many were third generation Malagasy-Chinese. Although mixed marriages were common, many continued to speak Cantonese. They seemed to do well and Chinese restaurants were seen in all the main cities and often on the main streets. Many also ran hotels, provision shops and supermarkets.

Indians and Pakistanis were spread all over Madagascar as well. They ran the retail sector of this country, and together with the Chinese, were sometimes called the 19th tribe of Madagascar.

After Fianarantsoa, we travelled on an awful stretch of extremely muddy road, to the Ranomafama National Park, where the rainforest contained more lemurs and other tropical species. As Southeast Asians, we were not overly thrilled by the rainforest, although we were delighted to see ayes-ayes with their sharp glowing eyes in the dark, chameleons, geckos, civet cats and more of other species of lemurs. Amidst the excitement, it was easy for one to forget momentarily that even in this supposed paradise of wildlife, uncontrolled logging had turned more than half of the national park, mostly in the deep jungles to the north, into an environmental wasteland.

***

Across Madagascar, we came across banners and advertisements with the words 'Tiko — Vita Malagasy', meaning 'Tiko — Malagasy-made'. These advertised products of the Tiko Group, the largest conglomerate in Madagascar, founded and owned by President Marc Ravalomanana. Ravalomanana grew up poor but was educated by missionaries in his home village not far from Tana. He completed his secondary education in Sweden in a strict Protestant school, and went on to establish his first business — home-made yoghurt — in his 20s. His business acumen served him well and his business grew rapidly as Madagascar liberalised its economy. Before long, his Tiko empire had come to control milk, yoghurt and all diary products in Madagascar, as well as interests in the mass media, television stations, soft drinks, and food and beverage products.

He then decided that he had an interest in politics and ran for mayor in Tana. As mayor, he won the hearts of the citizens by cleaning up the streets and tackling crime. Then he ran for the presidency in December 2001, which his supporters said he won. Incumbent President Ratsiraka refused to recognise the results and a six-month long political crisis ensued. As an old rat in power for almost two decades, Ratsiraka had the upper hand initially as he had the support of all the provincial governors except for that of Tana, and they imposed a blockade on the capital and the Central Highlands. Many in Tana and the large cities saw Ratsiraka as a corrupt dictator who had been in power for too long — Tobi pointed out an enormous fantasy palace complex that Ratsiraka had built for himself south of the capital. Chaos followed as bridges were blown up and clashes occurred between supporters of Ratsiraka and Ravalomanana. Ravalomanana declared himself president and set up a government in Tana, while Ratsiraka set up his own headquarters, rival government and central bank in his hometown, Toamasina. Economic activities came to a stop.

In June, however, the tide turned as the provinces fell one by one to Ravalomanana. Eventually, Ratsiraka fled for Paris while Ravalomanana's supporters marched into Toamasina. The political crisis ended, but the economic progress made in the last decade had all but been totally wiped out. Tourism had disappeared and foreign direct investments in the textile industry, one of Madagascar's largest, had dried up as well.

Madagascar is now recovering and perhaps its entrepreneurial president will be able to accelerate this process.

***

We travelled northwards through Madagascar's wine country — we tasted fairly good red wine but wondered about its consistency — and the land of the Betsileo, supposedly the best farmers of Madagascar who are famous for their terraced fields on the mountain slopes. The Betsileo were mostly Christians but also continued to practise some of their traditional customs and beliefs. They had a tradition of education and the relative (I stress relative) prosperity of the region was evidenced by large farmhouses that looked somewhat European from afar but were actually made of mud bricks and grass roofs.

Tobi's sharp eyes spotted a grand house-warming ceremony in which hundreds of guests were involved. We saw the locals dancing and merry-making, and then witnessed an exciting zebu fight. Six frightened zebus were rounded up into a ring, which was actually a hole dug into the ground, and a few hundred people crowded around it to watch the fun. A dozen brave, more likely reckless, young men jumped into the ring to attack the zebus with their bare arms. Some jumped onto the zebus while others agitated the sharp-horned zebus by waving blankets in an aggressive manner, not unlike the Spanish matador in front of an enraged bull. Enraged, some zebus charged at the attackers with their long intimidating horns, but most of the time, the zebus were terrified and headed for the ring gate instead, struggling to knock the door over. The men guarding the entrance held the gate tight to prevent the zebus from escaping, while shouting orders to the attackers behind the zebus. There were obviously some rules in the game, for once in a while an elder would reprimand some of the attackers for breaking certain rules, and they would then be obliged to leave the ring. A pity we did not understand Malagasy and that Tobi was taking a break in the car, which was a hundred metres of muddy path away.

After an interval, an elder would make some announcement and the zebus would be freed and guided out of the ring, and shortly after, the zebu fight would be repeated. After two hours, it seemed that the

Zebu fight held to celebrate a house-warming.

Fishing Malagasy highland style.

finale was approaching. This time, a few elders and women entered the ring as well. An elder had a branch of leaves and a bowl of sacred rum with him. After some chasing and herding the zebus around the ring, he selected a black and white zebu by splashing the sacred rum on it using the branch of leaves. The selected zebu, for some unknown reason, decided to jump onto a female zebu and tried to copulate with it. The crowd roared with laughter. The company in the ring had to beat the oversexed zebu off the female, and then led the other zebus out of the ring, leaving only the selected one.

The crowd had been waiting for this moment and indicated their approval of the selection by clapping. A few young men jumped into the ring to help. They chased the poor creature around for a while, then pinned it down and tied its limbs. A hole was dug into the ground next to the throat of the zebu and a vast vase placed inside the hole. Another elderly gentleman came forward with a huge, sharp knife. The crowd roared again and clapped. He uttered some prayers, positioned the knife on the animal's throat and then slit it.

First, a trickle of blood flowed into the vase, which soon turned into a bright red fountain spurting out in a spectacular though gory

The lemur, the icon of Madagascar.

fashion. The crowd cheered to indicate their approval. The vase of blood was then raised from the ground carefully and brought to the new house, while the butcher proceeded to cut up the zebu to distribute its meat to the honoured guests. At the new house, the blood was poured into zebu horns hollowed into a kind of drinking vessel, and then poured into different parts of the building for heavenly blessing.

The dancing continued, and in an even wilder state, following the distribution of the zebu meat and the rum having been passed around. At this moment, we decided to leave as we were running late and the sky was turning cloudy.

**

We headed north, passing the wood-carving town of Ambositra and then spent the night in Antsirabe, Madagascar's 'industrial belt', where there were a number of foreign investments. Here, we visited the market town of Betafo nearby, as well as a few lakes. It was here in the heartlands of the Malagasy people that deforestation and erosion were at their worst. There were few trees and everywhere we saw bare rolling hills and roadside stalls selling branches and leaves as burning fuel (properly matured trees had long been felled and only branches and shrubs were left). Even by the bank of Lac Andraikiba, where French colonials once spent summer holidays at the then fashionable Club Nautique under the shade of enormous fig trees and traveller's palms, not a single tree was left standing apart from a few ugly stumps. A rusty jump-stairs and a small-dilapidated building were all that remained of the Club. After the French departed, everything had fallen apart and was consumed by the tropical rainforest. Even the trees were dying and the animals disappearing fast.

We visited a metal pot factory where used metal was melted at high heat to be reused and remoulded into pots. The entire process was manual and antiquated, and the place — dirty, messy, cramped and polluted — looked like a scene from a Charles Dickens' novel from the time of the Industrial Revolution. No electricity was used at all, like many of this country's cottage industries and workshops, as it was expensive and unreliable. We did a quick computation to assess the profitability of this enterprise. Productivity was low here, with only 40 pots made every day. Given that the pots were sold for about US$7 and GDP per capita was US$870, we estimated that the factory made a margin of above 20%.

I wondered why China-made pots had not wiped out small plants like this — a standard Chinese plant was a lot more mechanised and probably manufactured 40,000 pots a day rather than 40. Perhaps shipping costs were high, but I was sure that the day shipping cost fell below a certain level, manual operations like this one would be wiped out. Already, most of the things I saw in the markets, including clothing, blankets (which formed part of the everyday apparel here as the locals walked around wrapped in blankets), bags and miscellaneous electrical appliances were already being made in China. I wondered when this factory would be hit. Or perhaps the margins were simply not enough for the Chinese exporter, thus the reluctance to enter this market. The economic rise of China has already had an impact on the global competitive landscape. Suddenly, many small countries have found themselves being rendered uncompetitive. If nothing was done to boost their competitiveness, their citizens might find themselves returning to subsistence farming.

We spent a night in Tana and then visited Périnet Special Reserve of the Andasibe-Mantadia National Park. We spent the afternoon walking around without seeing the one-metre tall indri with their incredible white and black fur, the greatest of the lemur. What a disappointment! We returned the next morning and this time we found two families of five individuals each, each group controlling a territory of about 15 hectares. The indri is famous for its early morning haunting calls, audible from 3km away, which initially frightened early European visitors who thought that the place was haunted.

After Pèrinet, we returned to Tana and visited the old Rova of

Ambohimanga in the countryside. This was an overpriced World Heritage site (with a US$5 entrance fee), with a dilapidated and half-bare palace surrounded by a simple wall. The larger and newer Rova of Tana had been burned down and all that remained was this one on Blue Hill.

***

Then it was back to Tana for two nights, before we flew to Mauritius and then Singapore. Walking around Tana and seeing the mass poverty and pathetic state of affairs around me, I was reminded of the story of the indri, known to the Malagasy as Babakoto. The Malagasy people believe that there was once a man named Koto, who left the village with his son to collect honey but failed to return. The villagers sent out a search party which could not find the two but instead found two indris looking at them from the trees. The villagers rationalised that the two had probably turned into the indris and hence called the indris Babakoto, meaning 'Papa Koto'.

Due to the supposed human origins of the indri, eating the indri is *fady*, or taboo. For a long time, the *fady* had helped the indri to survive. The indri used to be found all over the Highlands as well as the East

Coast. It was said that one could hear the cry of the indri from Toamasina to Tana, but it has become seriously endangered, found in large numbers only in the Périnet Special Reserve. Population pressure, deforestation and the loss of respect for the old cultural and traditional norms have led to the destruction of Madagascar's natural environment, caused erosion and threaten the country's agricultural sector as well as its long-term development and sustainability. Corruption and political instability have also made this country unattractive to foreign investors.

The fate of Madagascar is said to be linked to that of the indri. The question is how long the indri will continue to cry from the forests of Périnet.

POSTSCRIPT:

The prospects of Madagascar as an African tiger under its tycoon president disappeared in 2009, when President Marc Ravalomanana was overthrown in a coup d'etat, almost sparking off a civil war. Political uncertainty and stalemate is continuing to plague this country and tourists are ignoring the country amidst news of chaos.

Zebu Fight in Madagascar

Crowds gather to celebrate the completion of a new house.

A pre-fight feast was underway while visitors danced to traditional music to celebrate the joyous occasion.

Zebus were then marched into a fight pit.

Crowds soon built up around the pit as the fight was about to begin.

The fight began after all the bulls were marched into the pit. Young men jumped into the pit and began their attacks on the frightened creatures.

A few were cornered.

This unfortunate zebu was captured and tied.

And then sacrificed to the gods and the meat distributed to guests.

LATIN AMERICA

Guyana, Suriname & French Guiana — Land of Many Waters (2008)

Guiana is an Amerindian-Arawak word for 'Land of Many Waters', which appropriately describes the northwestern coast of South America, characterised first by wide rivers gushing down, deep tropical rainforests and then relatively flat coastal swampy plains. The Spanish, Portuguese, Dutch, French and British had all fought over these lands during their search for the legendary land of gold, El Dorado. But the deadly malarial swamps and failure to find valuable minerals did not create sufficient incentive for the powers to develop the land as intensively as they did elsewhere in the New World.

Unlike elsewhere in the Americas, the colonisers could not entice large numbers of European immigrants to settle in this hot, humid land. African slaves were first brought to work in the plantations, built on land created after the draining of the swamps by the Dutch. Later, the British brought Indians, Chinese and Portuguese as indentured workers to their part of the Guianas, and the Dutch brought Indians, Chinese and Javanese. Chinese and Vietnamese merchants came with the French and sprinkled French Guiana with general stores and Asian restaurants.

Today, the Guianas — although bearing broadly similar demographic landscape — is politically divided into three: the English-speaking Republic of Guyana (which is the local Creole word for Guiana), Dutch-speaking Republic of Suriname (named after an ancient tribe which lived here in pre-colonial days) and the French region of Guyane (commonly known as French Guiana in English).

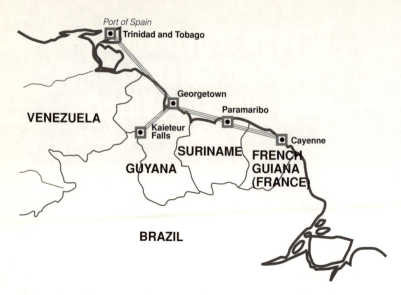

Guyana: The Dangers & Beauty of Georgetown

On one horribly humid evening, I flew into Georgetown, the capital of Guyana, from Port of Spain in Trinidad and Tobago. By the time I reached the Rima Guesthouse in central Georgetown on an ancient taxi which looked as though it would disintegrate any time, I was embarrassingly wet with perspiration. Furthermore, it was already past 9pm — not an ideal time to arrive in Georgetown; a poor, run-down and very dangerous town notorious for robbery and kidnapping. Fortunately, the guesthouse owner was waiting for me. I did not quite fancy walking around Georgetown at this hour looking for a place to stay. I was somewhat hungry, but would have to make do with some biscuits which had turned soft.

The presidential palace and prime minister's official residence were less than 100 metres away, and yet, I was warned by the guesthouse owner not to be on the streets before 8am or after 7pm. "Bad guys would recognise you as a foreigner and they would attack," she said. Indeed, the *Rough Guide to South America* suggests that one should get a cab even to travel to the next block at night. If the robbers didn't get you, the many coverless manholes on the unlit streets might, I reckoned.

Guyana was once considered a promising land with rich mineral wealth and natural resources. With a small population but a fair bit of bauxite, gold and sugar, it was thought that the country would emerge prosperous following independence in 1966. However, Guyana's then-President Burnham pursued socialist policies that alienated many. In 1970, he declared the country a 'Co-operative Republic' and turned the country into a one-party state.

The country nationalised all businesses and pursued self reliance as a national doctrine. The end result was economic destitution and mass poverty. "Until 1992, we all had nothing to eat," said Shiva, a taxi driver. "We only ate what we could grow and farmers found to keep grain secretly were persecuted." During this period, 600,000 Guyanese emigrated overseas, mostly to New York, Canada and the UK. Compare this to Guyana's current population of only 750,000 and one would realise the severity of the exodus.

Burnham's Guyana also actively pursued relations with the Soviet Bloc and the so-called Non-Aligned Movement. A monument with bronze busts of the four greats of the Non-Aligned Movement — Nasser of Egypt, Nehru of India, Tito of Yugoslavia and Nkrumah of

The ornate timber buildings of Georgetown, Guyana.

Ghana — still stands in a small garden at the heart of Georgetown. This tiny green patch is meticulously taken care of, in contrast to the dilapidation and dirt of downtown Georgetown. "Burnham ditched British Leyland buses and asked Nehru for some Indian buses instead. The buses came but they broke down in no time," said Chico, a Guyanese tour guide.

Burnham died in 1985 and by 1992, democracy was restored. Since then, Guyana has been opening its door to the outside world but the long term negative impact of the old socialist experiment will take a long time to shake off. Unemployment remains high in this small country and gangs terrorise the population with impunity. In fact, Guyana entered world headlines when a gang chieftain attacked the police headquarters in the capital, then massacred more than 20 people in two small towns, after accusing the police of arresting his 18 year-old pregnant girlfriend and killing a few of his gang members. This gang was even involved in the murder of a cabinet minister. It seemed like the government of Guyana could hardly do anything to the gangsters!

Dangers aside, Georgetown is an interesting city with a surprising number of monumental buildings made purely from timber — the 44-metre-high St George's Cathedral (one of the world's tallest wooden buildings), the Supreme Court, Stabroek Market, State House (presidential palace), residence of the prime minister and the city engineer's office. "Guyana is the treasure house of tropical wood and we have to flaunt it," said Chico.

Guyana has applied for World Heritage status for Georgetown's historical centre and I have no doubt they would eventually obtain that recognition. The lack of funds hinders conservation efforts. According to Chico, the beautiful old Portuguese cathedral was burnt down in fire three years ago. All that remained were the intricately carved metal grilling of its outer perimeters, which still stood on what could have been prime land in capital cities elsewhere.

Guyana was first colonised by the Dutch, who drained the swamps, dug canals and built a seawall to protect Georgetown, which is located on land 7 feet below sea level. Today's Georgetown is little changed from those old days. Cows grazing on the many deserted grass patches are scattered across town, alongside canals lined with Dutch wooden houses and sugar cane fields — a strange kind of tropical Holland, except that one has to be mindful of crime, malaria and dengue fever.

A Missionary-turned-Slave Trader From Singapore

Small Chinese-run shops selling food, household goods and merchandise are still found in some street corners around Georgetown. There used to be thousands of Chinese in Guyana. The first Chinese arrived in 1853 as indentured labourers from Guangdong. The long voyages from China to Guyana were horrendous, with many coolies dying even before they reached their destination. Many of those who survived the voyages and tough working conditions in the sugar plantations, however, remained in Guyana after the end of their indentures and some even married local Afro-Guyanese and Amerindians.

Led by a charismatic Chinese missionary from Singapore named O Tye Kim, a particular group not only converted many of the Chinese in Guyana, but also founded a river settlement named Hopetown in 1865. O was once a government surveyor in Singapore but supposedly found God after witnessing a dramatic sunset during which the sky was transformed into deep blood red and the sun obscured by strange clouds. After achieving success converting some Chinese in Singapore, he sailed to London alone, without his Singapore-born wife and three children, and convinced the Church Missionary Society there to finance his plans to convert Chinese immigrants in faraway Guyana.

Led by O, the settlement of Hopetown prospered initially as an agricultural settlement of free Chinese, later emerging as a charcoal manufacturing centre. O, however, was abruptly forced to resign from the spiritual and political leadership of the settlement when he was found to be having an affair with a local African woman who had become pregnant with his child. There were also accusations of embezzlement and extortion, as well as involvement in dodgy freewheeling deals that Hopetown had by then acquired a reputation for. He fled to a remote part of Guyana and was later reported to have emigrated to Trinidad around 1867.

Interestingly, O (now known as 'Tye Kim Orr') emerged again in Civil War-ravaged Louisiana that same year, together with a group of Cuban Chinese. Described variously as "the priest" and as a "Chinese gentleman whose enunciation was very clearly resembling very much that of an educated Spaniard", O became a respectable school teacher, who later went on a speaking circuit around the American South about the merits of employing Chinese coolies to replace the recently freed former Black slaves (whom O described as inherently lazy and undisciplined). It's amazing to see how a god-fearing Singapore Chinese missionary went to South America to found an idealistic community in the deep jungles, but eventually drifted to Cuba and then the American South to become a dodgy importer of Chinese slave-coolie labour.

The Chinese community in Guyana prospered — one Arthur Raymond Chung was a prominent lawyer, judge and eventually became the first ceremonial president of Guyana in 1970. During the chaotic 1970s and 1980s, however, many Chinese left Guyana, emigrating to the US, Canada or the UK. Today, about 2,000 ethnic Chinese live in Guyana, most of them new immigrants from Mainland China, who arrived in the last two decades. The memories of the Chinese pioneers in Guyana are largely forgotten, consigned mainly to dusty academic journals and faded photo albums scattered in the suburbs of New York, Toronto and London.

Kaieteur Falls: The World's Largest?

The British took over Guyana in 1803, and after the abolition of slavery, brought the Indians over as indentured workers, who still live largely in the huge rice fields, sugar cane plantations and vegetable farms of the coastal plains. The Afro-Guyanese, descendants of African slaves, concentrate mainly in Georgetown's many slums and shantytown suburbs. It was with an Indo-Guyanese émigré family, now residing in Canada, that I visited Guyana's most famous attraction, Kaieteur Falls.

It was David's first visit back to Guyana after leaving the country 25 years ago. "The country was bankrupt then, from those silly communist policies. It is only now beginning to stand up again," said David, who as an Indo-Guyanese Canadian, has complicated multi-faceted identities like many overseas Chinese — from the potentially differing country of one's passport, one's country of birth and one's most original ancestral roots. David also remembered some of his joyous innocent days in Guyana. "We trekked the jungles when we were young, and we saw five types of jaguars and great cats, as well as numerous varieties of colourful and loud macaws and parrots."

Kaieteur Falls, located deep in Guyana, is supposedly the world's

Kaieteur Falls,
Guyana from the sky.

largest single drop waterfall, i.e. it has the largest volume of water —
663 cubic metres per second, falling over a height of 228 metres.
Situated in a deep ravine surrounded by almost impenetrable tropical
rainforest, it takes five days through very rough roads to get here
by land.

We took only an hour to get there — by flying on a six-seater
Cessna, with me in the co-pilot's seat — across the flat fertile Demerara
valley and then into the lush greenery of the Amazonian jungle. A freak
storm rocked the plane as we flew above the jungle canopy. Visibility
dropped significantly and I could only chant, "*Om mani padme om, om
mani padme om ...*" Suddenly, a ray of light tunnelled through the darkness
of clouds and rain, and we found ourselves approaching a ravine, with
a gush of silvery water pouring down a vertical wall of rocks beyond.
The magnificent Kaieteur!

We walked around the various viewpoints, admiring this gorgeous
work of Mother Earth. We also saw a golden frog, whose poison is
reserved by the local Amerindians for their enemies and dangerous
anacondas. The national park guide also added that the poison could
also be used as a sex potion, and its effects had been proven to be many
times more powerful than the Viagra.

***

A sparsely populated country like Guyana faces risks from land-hungry
neighbours. Venezuela to the west has a historical claim to all lands
to the west of the Essequibo River, i.e. three quarters of all Guyana
territory. In 1899, an international arbitration tribunal awarded most
of the disputed land to British Guiana, now Guyana, in a decision
that was accepted by both Venezuela and Britain in 1905. However, in
1962, on the basis of a posthumous publication of a book by a junior
member of the 1899 arbitration team (in which he alleged unfair
British pressure and interference), the old claim was revived and the
arbitration award set aside. Even today, the issue remains unresolved.

As a Guyanese driver said, "If oil is suddenly discovered in the Essequibo," which is actually quite possible according to recent reports, "crazy Chavez's Venezuela would just march in and tiny Guyana would not be able to do anything." Sounds very much like the Iraq-Kuwait story.

On my journey to the airport to fly to Suriname, I met Sammy, a friendly Indo-Guyanese taxi driver. A balding man about 60 years old, Sammy was aghast that I had not seen Guyana apart from Georgetown and Kaieteur, and I hadn't tried the Guyanese delicacies — pepper pot and cooked up rice. "You should give yourself more time. If you are not leaving today, I would cook you some Guyanese food and show you the beautiful countryside," Sammy said.

Would you swap Manhattan for Suriname?

From Georgetown, I got on a Brazilian regional airline — Meta Airlines — to Paramaribo, the exotic capital of the neighbouring Dutch-speaking republic of Suriname, once known as Dutch Guiana. Paramaribo, Paramaribo, Paramaribo... what gets more exotic than this? Like Timbuktu and Ouagadougou, Paramaribo is one of those places in the world you should visit, even if it is just for the name. It was once attractive enough for the Dutch to exchange the tiny cold island of Manhattan for (with the British), in one of the worst real estate deals ever done in history. The deal had its logic — Manhattan was a miserably cold island besieged by vicious Indian tribes, but Suriname was a land of green gold — sugar plantations that fetched wealth and glory to build beautiful merchant palaces in Amsterdam and Utrecht. Everything is easier with the benefit of hindsight.

Paramaribo is today the capital of Suriname, which at 165,000 sq km is an even more sparsely populated country than Guyana. Suriname has only 500,000 inhabitants and an émigré population of 400,000 living in the Netherlands. Graceful Dutch civic buildings and traders' houses next to venerable ancient trees lined the roads and streets of this UNESCO World Heritage city. Paramaribo certainly looked more beautiful and wealthier than Guyana. There were more shops, and they were better stocked than those in Guyana. Nor were there potholes and uncovered manholes on sidewalks.

Suriname is one of the world's ethnically most diverse countries. Indians (also brought here as indentured workers in the 19th century) and Creoles (descendants of African slaves, with some European mix) each account for about 30% of the population, while Indonesians (brought here by the Dutch), Maroons (descendants of escaped African slaves who intermarried with Amerindians), and Amerindians and Chinese make up the remaining.

Upon arrival, I had my passport checked by a Creole officer, money changed by a Dutch bank officer, was driven to the city by a Javanese, bought a bottle of mineral water from a Chinese shop, had Indonesian *mee goreng* Surinamese style cooked by a Javanese and a strange nice white herbal drink made by Amerindians to ease digestion. The sugar I had for my breakfast coffee probably came from an Indian-run sugar plantation.

The Chinese in Trinidad, Guyana and Suriname, as well as French Guiana, run almost all the supermarkets and general stores, and a large proportion of retail business of any sort. Like anywhere else, there are two major categories of Chinese — the descendants

A magnificent mosque in Paramaribo: Multi-ethnic and multi-religious Suriname is also the home of many Indian and Javanese Muslims.

of 19th century indentured workers, and the new immigrants from Mainland China who arrived in the last two decades. With the rise of China as an economic power, it is increasingly the second category of Chinese, i.e. newcomers, that play a greater role in the economies of these countries.

In Suriname, I was told that the Chinese built many of the good roads in the last decade. Tired of the many demands and conditions made by the Dutch for developmental loans, the Suriname government told the Dutch to keep their cash. The Surinamese went to the Chinese instead and got multi-billion dollar interest-free loans with ten-year repayment terms. And more importantly, no political or social conditions attached. "We are glad that there is now competition with the Europeans. The Chinese now have the biggest embassy in Suriname, even larger than the Dutch and American embassies, and we are happy about that," said a Surinamese businessman.

Despite this, not everything had gone smoothly for the Chinese. I was told about a Chinese plan to turn a patch of rainforest into palm oil plantations. The timber chopped down in the clearing of the jungle would be sold to China and thousands of Surinamese would find employment in the oil palm plantations. However, environmentalists rallied against the proposal and the Maroons, who lived in those parts, said their sacred places would be desecrated by the plantations. Don't you dare mess with the Maroons. Descendants of escaped slaves who intermarried with Amerindians, they are a hardy lot who set up self-governing chieftains and fought off many Dutch attacks. Even as late as the 1980s, a Maroon guerrilla force brought the country's economy and development to a standstill. Needless to say, the plan was torpedoed.

One of Suriname's biggest obstacles to development is the lack of a credible population size for industrial development. A second proposal involves bringing in 30,000 Chinese immigrants who would revive dozens of abandoned or disused plantations, and indirectly set up a whole infrastructure to export the produces of the revived plantations.

Sounds like an excellent plan to exploit the business acumen and 'invisible hand' of the entrepreneurial Chinese, Adam Smith style. Furthermore, it is about the revival of old plantations, not the establishment of new ones that could potentially damage the environment. Not surprisingly, there is also a lot of opposition. "There is a lot of drug interest in this country, many of whom are against having so many newcomers poking into remote areas and discovering the drug smuggling that is going on," said a Surinamese I met.

Suriname, like many Central and South American countries, has become a conduit for drug trafficking, either to the US or to Europe via Netherlands, where there is a huge Surinamese émigré community. The many casinos along the waterfront, I was told, serve as money laundering venues for drug money. While having *nasi goreng* (Indonesian fried rice) breakfast at a downtown café, a sneaky mestizo-looking man with crumpled dirty-green shirt joined me at my table and asked where I was from. When told I was from Singapore, he said he once had a good Singaporean friend while living in Amsterdam.

He then whispered into my ear, "Henry used to bring me *bai-fen* from Thailand, and he gave me some as a friend, plus excellent roast pork slices from Singapore." *Bai-fen* is the Mandarin word for cocaine.

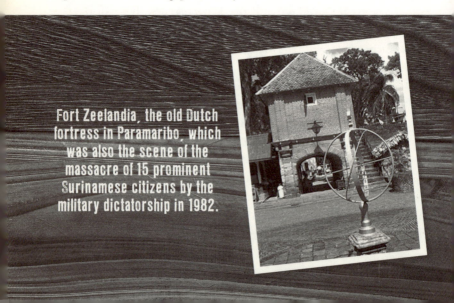

Fort Zeelandia, the old Dutch fortress in Paramaribo, which was also the scene of the massacre of 15 prominent Surinamese citizens by the military dictatorship in 1982.

He went on and on about how he liked the friendlier Singapore Chinese and disliked Chinese from China, whom he described as cunning. And he asked me to buy him a glass of orange juice, "It's not expensive, can you? Henry bought me drinks all the time." By then, I had finished my *nasi goreng* and coffee, and made my move. "Sorry sir, I'm not Henry and I've got to go."

In fact, the trial of Desi Bouterse, a former military dictator and convicted drug smuggler, for the 1982 murder of 15 prominent Surinamese citizens opposed to the military regime, was soon to begin. Bouterse was the mastermind of not one, but two coups, including one in 1992 during which Bouterse ordered the government to step down by phone, hence the so-called 'Telephone Coup'. He was found guilty of cocaine trafficking by a court in The Netherlands in 1999, but has remained free in Suriname. Given his continual influence in the military and his enormous wealth, it remains to be seen if he would ever to taken to account by any court.

While making enquiries about transit to French Guiana, I met Wilfred, the friendly owner of a group of transportation, bus and travel businesses. I showed him my website and told him about my travels round the world. He drove me around, showing me the sights of this beautiful city and its many diverse architectural styles. "This is a great country with so much to offer. But the infrastructure has to be built. More hotels, good ones, and better roads."

As Wilfred spoke, Dutch tourists were frolicking in the pool of Torarica, the best hotel in town where we had *mee soto* Indonesian style and Creole fried rice topped with chicken and tapioca paste, and a few Mainland Chinese in their 30s — the sort who looked like professionals or consultants rather than the typical plump middle-age official type — were tanning on the sun decks next to the pool. "But we also need more sensible policies, like getting rid of visas for the 400,000 Dutch of Surinamese origin," he said.

My counterpoint to that would be, Suriname should abolish visas for those countries who have a higher per capita GDP and unlikely to overstay in the country. I know of Australians who want to come to Suriname but have no way of getting a visa because there is no Surinamese embassy in Australia or most places for that matter (Singaporeans do not need a visa for Suriname but many other countries do). Countries that are more interested in developing the tourism industry and economy in general should put aside their nationalist pride and traditional insistence on reciprocity for visa waiver. Only with higher income and the international respectability that follows growing wealth, will a country's citizens enjoy visa waivers across the world.

French Guiana: Dodgy River Crossing

Along near-deserted roads through rainforests, I moved on to Cayenne, the capital of French Guiana (Guyane in French), from Suriname. French Guiana is the last vestige of European colonialism in Mainland South America. In fact, it is constitutionally part of France — not a colony or overseas territory — and part of the European Union. It uses the Euro as currency and its map is featured on all Euro banknotes, at the bottom of each reverse side.

It took me 7 hours to get here from Paramaribo. It wasn't so much the time that mattered, but the anxiety involved. Firstly, it had not occurred to me that the authorities in French Guiana officially required a Yellow Fever Certificate from visitors and I only learnt about it while reading my guidebook in greater detail while in Suriname. My new Surinamese friend, Wilfred, warned me that people have been disallowed entry into French Guiana when found that they did not have the certificate.

I had left my Yellow Fever certificate at home. I contemplated getting another certificate in Paramaribo but that would only be available on Wednesday mornings (it was Thursday when I realised this), and I had to get to Cayenne to catch a flight to Martinique before that. With the hope that I could persuade French border officials that I had taken the Yellow Fever vaccination, I printed a copy of an old blog entry in which I mentioned the vaccinations I had to take. The blog also contained photos of the cover of the vaccination booklets.

Fortunately, the friendly French border officials did not ask for the vaccination certificate and instead stamped my passport without any fuss. Hurrah! Given the tight schedule I had, my trip would have been in a mess if they didn't allow me to enter Guiana.

Secondly, even before getting my passport stamped by the French, I was really nervous of the chaotic situation that prevailed at the Suriname-French border, basically a wide river full of small canoes ferrying people across. I arrived at this riverbank after a two-hour journey in a cramped shared taxi where I was squeezed between a fat Surinamese man carrying a huge cage with a noisy black bird in his lap and a petite Colombian hairdresser with dyed blonde locks, only to be mobbed by half a dozen aggressive black men soliciting for passengers for their canoes — two of whom were already having a tug of war over my luggage. I shouted for them to stop (while secretly trembling with fear), as I had to get my passport stamped by Suriname Immigration.

This river might be full of people crossing the international border, but 99.9% of them did so without bothering about passport stamps. Some of these Surinamese have dual Dutch nationality and

thus as EU citizens have every right to enter French territory without formalities. The rest of the Surinamese and all sorts of South American nationalities I saw at the border simply crossed over to work at the French side illegally.

The French don't give a damn because firstly, French Guiana, one-sixth the size of France in surface area, is very thinly populated with only 250,000 inhabitants, and thus illegals doing dirty work is unofficially tolerated. Secondly, French Guiana is surrounded by the Atlantic Ocean on its northern side, and by the deep jungles of poor Suriname and Brazil on the other three sides. So anyone who gets into French Guiana is stuck there. No danger of them moving on to France proper or Europe.

I had to ensure that I got a proper Suriname exit stamp so that the French Immigration would stamp an entry permit on my passport. The problem was, because few people had ever bothered about getting the Suriname stamp, the Suriname Immigration was located some distance away from the riverside where the action took place. I had to beg the taxi driver to bring me to the Immigration, which was something he didn't have to do for the other passengers. We drove so far away from the riverbank that I half suspected I was about to get robbed. When we reached Suriname Immigration, the lazy, sleepy and shockingly shirtless officials there had to be pleaded to put on their uniform and stamp my passport.

Back at the riverbank, I got into a canoe full of passengers without a Suriname exit stamp and had no intention of getting a French entry stamp. The boatman, a tall loud black man who spoke a strange Creole-English mix, was also not overly enthusiastic in bringing me to the French Immigration quay. He disembarked the other passengers at a part of French riverbank full of waiting taxi drivers and took his own sweet time chatting to the other boatmen.

Even as he returned to the boat with another black man supposedly to bring me to French Immigration 200 metres away, it occurred to me that these aggressive, scruffy people looked perfectly capable of rowing the boat somewhere and then chopping me into pieces. I had my dark glasses on and tried to look fierce and impatient. Fortunately, all they did was to steer the boat to the French Immigration where I got my passport duly stamped. The only negative thing was he demanded twice as much boat fare as earlier agreed, I suppose for the additional journey he had to make for my passport stamping. I was relieved when I finally got into the shared taxi for Cayenne.

What a day!

***

Kourou, some 50 kilometres away, is where the Arianne rocket of the European Space Agency is launched. The Guiana Space Centre was established because of its proximity to the Equator, which would substantially minimise the fuel load required to launch rockets. However, I only had one full Sunday here and the museum and launch centre were both closed.

I also contemplated visiting the infamous Devil Island near Kourou, where prominent prisoners of the French state were once imprisoned in very harsh conditions, but decided against it as the weather was awful and my kneecap, which now seemed to stir whenever it rained (could it be rheumatism?), had begun to hurt again.

In any case, it was a good decision to stay put in Cayenne, as I had unexpectedly come across the first weekend of the multiple-week Cayenne Carnival. Cayenne's citizens were all out on the streets celebrating with the masqueraded marchers who were in the most colourful, exuberant costumes. The local resident Brazilian and Haitian contingents were among the most joyous contingents and I had a field time photographing them all.

***

I stayed two nights in Cayenne before heading for Martinique, another French overseas department in the Caribbean. It was a very wet weekend with intermittent showers. Most of the shops and restaurants were, like those in Guyana and Suriname, run by Chinese. I had a late lunch at a Chinese café — tasty croissants and coffee at a fraction of the price charged by cafes run by the local Europeans and Creoles — and chatted to their Hangzhou-born owners. Since I did not speak French and had difficulty understanding the hotel staff, the local Chinese provided me with some useful tips. Increasingly during my travels, I have found the new Chinese immigrants, now found even in the most remote towns in exotic lands, a useful connection in navigating new places. And with that, I departed from good old Guianas, and headed for the French Caribbean.

Postscript:

Guyana and French Guiana have hobbled along. In August 2010, Desi Bouterse, the old military dictator and convicted drug smuggler, was elected President of Suriname — a move that would made it even more impossible for him to be charged in court.

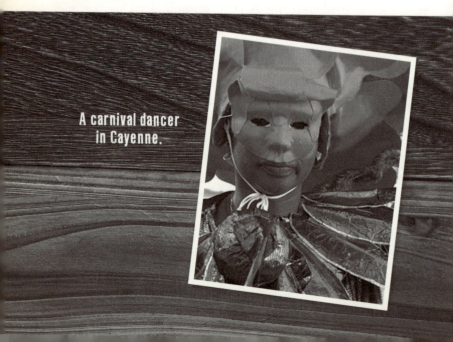

A carnival dancer in Cayenne.

Venezuela —
Angel Falls, Mysterious Tepuis
& the Andes
(2009)

When a group of Spanish conquistadors arrived on the northern coast of the South American continent in 1499, they saw natives living in houses on stilts over water. Hence, they called this territory Venezuela, meaning 'Little Venice'. But the name Venezuela is a misnomer, for it is a vast country of varied and dramatic landscapes, spread over a territory twice the size of California. Over two weeks, my friends and I would crisscross Venezuela via planes, buses, cars and even boats, across deep Amazonian tropical rainforests, boundless savannah plains, mysterious tabletop mountains, fertile green valleys and even the high Andes.

We arrived in a Venezuela full of huge billboards extolling President Hugo Chavez's 21st century Bolivarian Socialist Revolution. State and municipal councils proclaim their support for a dramatic transformation of Venezuelan society in favour of the working class, who according to Chavez, have long been suffering and exploited by the oligarchs. Since coming to power in 1998, the former paratrooper has not only changed the country's official name (from Republic of Venezuela to the Bolivarian Republic of Venezuela) to proclaim his support for the ideals of Venezuela's founding father, Simon Bolivar, but also its time zone, flag and coat of arms.

Chavez had claimed that time zones were 'created by imperialists' and setting clock back by half an hour would allow school children to wake up under natural light. A new star has been added to the flag and arms to pay tribute to Simon Bolivar, and the head of the galloping horse currently on the coat of arms was switched from right to left. Chavez said that his daughter had asked why the horse was galloping with its head tossed backward, instead of facing the future in a natural direction. Based on research, he discovered that the existing horse is an 'imperialist horse' designed by a British diplomat, and it was "a horse being reined in, someone is holding him back, they put him looking into the past".

So the arms and flag have been changed accordingly so that the horse now inspires the nation to move forward to the future. A sarcastic Venezuelan we met said he would rather the president spend more time increasing everybody's well-being and income levels than changing the country's name, time zone and national symbols. According to a skeptical news report, all these were part of 'Chavez's drive to put his mark on every aspect of the country's national identity'.

Caracas, the federal capital of Venezuela, is located in a fertile valley squeezed between two mountain ranges parallel to the country's Caribbean coast. Venezuela is the fifth largest oil exporter in the world, and its wealth has enabled the country to build a modern motorway network, complete with long tunnels through the many tall mountains that cut across the country. Skyscrapers of blinking lights form the

One of the many political posters one sees across Chavez's Venezuela.

silhouette of this city of five million inhabitants. But it is also evident that many in Venezuela have not benefited from the oil bonanza, and some of the lights we saw were those of the many shantytowns surrounding Caracas.

The vast majority of the population lives below poverty level and we found topless hustlers waving at passing cars just opposite the steel-and-glass headquarters of the Venezuelan state petroleum company, PDVSA. Caracas is also the murder capital of the world, well ahead of Johannesburg, Cape Town and Port Moresby. In fact, with 34 murders a day, Venezuela's homicide rate approximates that of war-torn Iraq, which according to the Frontpage Magazine, is 'the rough equivalent of the lives snuffed out by a typical suicide bombing in Iraq; its population is about the same size as Venezuela's 27 million'.

Some analysts say that like Nigeria, Venezuela suffers from the 'oil malaise' — the country benefits so much from occasional spike in oil prices that there is little incentive to build other industries. Instead, everything is imported with the easy money that comes with the oil. As we drove through the fashionable neighbourhood of Las Mercedes, I could not help but notice how American the whole place looked. Huge classy malls, branded boutiques, fast food outlets, huge cars… all the symbols of a mass consumer society.

We had a free day in Caracas, where we explored sites downtown relating to Simon Bolivar, the 'Liberator' of not only Venezuela, but also of five other Latin American countries, namely Colombia, Panama, Ecuador, Peru and Bolivia, the last of which was named after him. Over a twenty year period, Bolivar defeated the armies of Spain and their supporters, as well as various local warlords, to set up the Gran Colombian federation. He dreamt of establishing a united pan-American state of free republics, but it did not take long before his federation fell apart. The states bickered and fought against each other. Even his native land, Venezuela, seceded from Gran Colombia and declared him *persona non grata*. He died from tuberculosis at the age of 37, a bitter and broken man.

It was only years after his death that Bolivar, the legend and demigod, was resurrected. In Venezuela, the heart of every city, town and village has a Plaza Bolivar, and streets, buildings and organisations were named after him. President Chavez brought Bolivar-mania to new heights, by proclaiming his ideals as the official state ideology and naming the country after him. He nationalised not only PDVSA and major industrial corporations and supermarkets, but sought to distribute wealth among the poor. We visited the National Pantheon where the remains of Bolivar and other Venezuelan national heroes were interred, and admired the impressive array of huge flags of nations liberated by Bolivar.

Yet there was another sign that Chavez's Bolivarian Revolution was not proceeding well. Here, a haggled-looking man who spoke good US-accented English tried to persuade us to employ him as a guide. He was a graduate of Oklahoma University but lost his senior engineer job a few years ago. There are few jobs in Venezuela today and many middle-class Venezuelans have emigrated abroad. How sad that dignified people like him had to tout on the streets for uncertain business.

We also visited UCV, the Central University of Venezuela. The university complex has an enormous campus that was planned and built in the 1950s in an exuberant modernist-art deco style, and modern sculptures are scattered through the premises. The whole complex was declared an UNESCO World Heritage Site in 2000 as an outstanding example of Modern Movement in architecture. The concept was perhaps grand and impressive then but the place, regrettably, looked dated and worn out. Rubbish was strewn across the area and paint was peeling off the walls. It was all very well to be inscribed onto this prestigious list, but maintenance is often a tougher job.

***

We proceeded to the city of Ciudad Bolivar in the east on an overnight bus. I found myself sitting beside a Mainland Chinese who was playing a 1990s Andy Lau CD to pass the night. Li, in his late 30s, had been in Venezuela for over 10 years and his thickly-accented Mandarin betrayed his peasant origins in the countryside of Guangdong Province. He thought we were oil engineers from Beijing, given the standard Mandarin we spoke. There have been quite a few in recent years, given President Chavez's close ties with China.

Li first came here to join relatives who had arrived a few years before him and set up a flourishing business. He now works for a friend's supermarket in the small city of El Tigre in the jungles of Guayana, eastern Venezuela. He has never gone home since, although he did switch a few jobs. Here, he also met and married a fellow Chinese and has two children who have Venezuelan citizenship. Li said there are Chinese shops and restaurants everywhere in Venezuela, even in the smallest villages — indeed I was to pass quite a few even in indescript dusty town in the remote east of the country. Life is tough, Li insisted. The local police are racist and corrupt, he added, and they frequently demanded money from Chinese they stopped on the streets.

He was curious why we flew all the way from Singapore to visit Venezuela. Is Angel Falls really worth seeing, he asked. Could you not find something similar elsewhere? To many Chinese who left their homeland for little-known faraway lands, travelling afar was an act of desperation. China, despite its rapid economic growth, does not offer sufficient opportunities for the less educated peasants farming on pathetically small parcels of land, and even what little they own is frequently taken over by corrupt officials and unscrupulous real estate developers out for a quick buck. We should consider ourselves lucky that our ancestors left China much earlier and we come here today as privileged tourists.

**

At Ciudad Bolivar, where the Liberator regrouped his armies and drafted his grand scheme for the Americas after a major defeat by Spanish forces, we had our first glimpse of the legendary Orinoco River, gateway to the Land of El Dorado. Enya's 1988 sensation, *Orinoco Flow*, rang in my ears:

Let me sail let me sail let the Orinoco Flow
Let me reach let me beach on the shores of Tripoli
Let me sail let me sail let me crash upon your shore
Let me reach, let me beach far beyond the Yellow Sea
Deh deh deh deh deh deh...
Sail away, sail away, sail away...

***

We flew on a Cessna 5-seater from Ciudad Bolivar to the remote Peman Indian Village of Canaima, which is also the gateway to the Canaima National Park, a UNESCO World Heritage Site. The over-30,000 sq km Canaima National Park, about the size of Belgium, contains not only Angel Falls — the world's tallest single drop waterfall at 979m — but also savannah grasslands (known as Gran Sabana), impenetrable Amazonian rain forests and numerous tepuis. The tepuis are mysterious table top mountains with their own unique ecosystems and endemic fauna and flora, and they have inspired books and movies such as *The Lost World* and *Jurassic Park*.

We were met at Canaima airport by our rather grouchy, uncommunicative Peman guide, Tony, and together with other tourists from Russia, China and the UK, we got onto a truck through a muddy track to a jetty behind one of the smaller falls of Canaima Lagoon. Then, on a motorised Indian boat, we headed for Angel Falls on Rio Churun, passing through initially rolling grasslands flanked in the horizons with awesome tepuis.

Angel Falls lies on the cliffside of Auyantepui ('Mountain of the God of Evil' in the Peman language), the largest of all tepuis. At over 700 sq km, the vertical massifs of Auyantepui are larger than all of Singapore and Rio Churun originates from the heights of the tepui and flows

The magnificent and mysterious tepuis of Southeastern Venezuela.

A scene from the canoe on the way to Angel Falls.

One of the many waterfalls and cataracts in Canaima National Park.

through it. Our boat entered Auyantepui through the appropriately named Canyon del Diablo ('Canyon of the Devil'). On both sides of the river were dense jungles that rose gradually to the forbidding vertical walls of the Canyon which towered above us. Occasional falls cascade off the misty cliffsides into the jungle canopy, but none of them approaching the grandeur of Angel Falls itself. Heavy rain came and went during the four-hour boat ride, not to mention the numerous rapids we rammed through. We were completely drenched by the time we reached Angel Falls.

Then it was a rigorous one-hour trek through the tropical jungle to reach the furthest viewpoint you could get to. My long-suffering kneecap complained non-stop, not to mention the loud mocking calls from unseen frogs, insects and unknown creatures in the jungle. There it was — the world's tallest fall in front of us! It is five times the height of Niagara Falls and twice that of Victoria Falls.

The night was spent at a camp on the opposite side of the river from the Falls. We had delicious rice and chicken for dinner. On hindsight, I wonder if the food was really tasty, or if I was hungry, wet and cold, and that anything warm would have tasted like manna from heaven. The whole place was sandy and dirty, and the mosquitoes' symphony orchestra played the whole night long. My camera was wet and began to malfunction. In fact, my camera would not work the whole of next morning. I was relieved when we finally left the camp.

***

Back in Canaima, we explored the many scenic waterfalls easily accessible from the Peman village where we stayed. *Jurassic Park* was filmed here, with the area's rolling plains and spectacular tepuis straddled in the surrounding landscape. The Pemans looked prosperous and seemed to own many of the tourist businesses here. The school buildings looked decent, clean and pleasant. There were no beggars that I saw throughout indigenous communities in South America. In fact, we were told that the Pemans are one of the most successful indigenous groups in taking advantage of tourism and benefiting from it.

We noticed that the Chinese tourists had no problem using their China Mobile to speak to people back home, whereas our cell phones and those of the other tourists did not seem to work here in this remote part of Venezuela (although our phones worked in Caracas). Perhaps this says a lot about the Chinese determination to extend their commercial reach throughout the world, and hence their mobile operators were willing to conclude more exhaustive roaming agreements with operators everywhere.

***

We flew to Santa Elena on yet another Cessna five-seater. This must have been my most frightening flight ever. We left Canaima in bright sunshine but found ourselves flying through three separate storms in the next hour and 20 minutes. Many a time we were flying between the vertical walls of tepuis rising much higher than us, with just mist, clouds and minimal visibility ahead. Below us was the deep dark green canopy of the Amazonian jungle — the sort of impenetrable labyrinth where wreckages of lost planes were discovered only many decades after their crashes.

Wind howled away and rain beat relentlessly against the metal sheets that made this tiny flying machine. There was one occasion when our plane literally stood still in the air, as we were up against winds in the opposite direction. And guess what? We were flown by a young trainee pilot with baby face and puffy hair, guided by a much more assuring trainer whom we guessed was his father, given their likeness and his affectionate pat over the younger man's shoulders. Even then, we prayed in silence through the episode. Santa Maria! With much relief, we reached Santa Elena safely... there was clear blue sky there, sunny, fresh and clear, and us totally shaken by the flight! Moments upon landing, the trainer turned and asked, "How was the flight? How did you find the landing?"

***

We were surprised to discover a new and modern airport at such a remote frontier town like Santa Elena. Our local travel agent had someone to pick us up and we had a brief drive-around this small city. Santa Elena was a busy town with many shops and restaurants, many of which have Chinese owners. In fact, the two most prominent restaurants at Plaza Bolivar are Chinese restaurants, complete with bright red lights and suspicious lanterns.

Santa Elena is an obvious beneficiary of a lively border trade. US dollars and Brazilian reales are the main currencies of this trade, and it was here that we got the most Venezuelan bolivars for a dollar. Six to the dollar was the Santa Elena rate, whereas we got only 4.5 on our first day in Venezuela, although most places in Venezuela, as we later came to realise, would do with about 5.5 to 5.8. The official exchange rate is only 2.15, a far cry from the black market rate. The black market rate occurs when governments start to print money to finance projects to spend beyond its means. This means the money isn't worth as much as it asserts. Unless the situation is reversed, it gets worse and worse, as the government begins to institute even more drastic capital control rules to prevent people from switching to a more valuable foreign 'hard' currency.

More often than not, countries with such capital controls tend to have major corruption issues as well, as officials attempt to profit from the situation by getting hard currency from the state at lower official rates and then selling the foreign currencies in the black market. As the Chavez administration nationalises an increasing number of businesses, it has to print money to finance such moves, even as oil prices increase. This depresses confidence in the bolivars, which exaggerates the gap between the official and black market rates.

During our stay in Venezuela, we didn't meet any Venezuelan with good things to say about Chavez, but this could be because the people we met were mostly the English-speaking elite and middle/upper class who dislike him intensely because these policies were populist and anti-rich in nature. They saw him as egoistic, dictatorial and communistic, and some considered him silly in wasting oil money for his grand projects and schemes to enhance Venezuelan prestige.

Many businessmen told me Chavez's policies have made business, planning and investment difficult. When we stopped by a gas station in Santa Elena to buy petrol, we encountered a long queue with some form of rationing going on. Some people might even have to use connections to get the petrol they need. When you see this in an oil-producing country, you know something is very wrong with the economy.

The country is full of political billboards and graffiti. They often depict Chavez, Simon Bolivar, the socialist star Che Guevara and other leftist figures. Many states and cities called themselves 'Bolivarian Socialist States' or 'Socialist City', which reminded me of Soviet slogans but with a Latin flavour. Even then, one cannot deny that Chavez has the support of many if not majority of the Venezuelans, at least up till recently and perhaps for a while still. Whatever it is, Venezuela has become a much polarised society.

***

Frank was our guide in the Gran Sabana region. He was originally from Caracas, came here for an adventure, loved the place and stayed on for over 30 years. He is a fourth generation Lebanese and like most Venezuelans, was constantly going crazy over women. He would always comment whenever we passed a pretty girl. On many occasions, he even stopped to pretend to ask for directions. One cannot fault him, for Venezuela is renowned for having the world's most beautiful women. Over the years, five Venezuelans have won the Miss World competition and the country has many schools dedicated to training girls to produce beauty pageant winners. Venezuela also has a thriving plastic surgery industry and we noticed, even within hours of arrival, that almost every other girl in Caracas had a rather huge bosom. We wonder how many of these were real, or mere artistic masterpieces of the country's plastic surgeons.

***

Alejandro Stern is a gold and diamond merchant in Santa Elena de Uairen. His office was a small non-descript one storey shop building on a side street of Santa Elena. There was not a lot outside except a sign that spelt his name and address, and another that noted that English is spoken. A bored man in his late 40s sat just outside the door, his pistol partially covered by his jacket.

Frank spoke briefly to the guard, then into the intercom device at the door. There was a window with dark glass on the wall next to the door — the sort that allows the people inside to see those outside but not the other way round. A buzz and then Frank turned the doorknob. We entered the small dark room.

A burly man with short white hair whom I estimated to be in his 50s sat at a dusty desk with a table lamp and piles of papers, and a few unfamiliar boxes and devices. This was a strange setting, definitely not the everyday jewelry shop one would expect. The only sign of the trade were a few posters with photos of gold crystals. The décor made it look like a home office of some sort but the atmosphere resembled that of Hollywood's impression of the office of a mafia chief's accountant.

"Welcome, I am Alejandro Stern. I trade in gold and diamond." He spoke in clear precise English, without any Venezuelan accent. And he obviously also traded stocks and currencies. Stern had a screen on the wall with jumping counters and currency quotes.

As it turned out, Stern was a fourth generation Venezuelan with English roots and had come to Santa Elena more than a decade ago, due to the rich deposits of minerals — specifically gold crystals and diamonds in the plains and jungles of the Gran Sabana. If Venezuela was the legendary land of El Dorado, then Gran Sabana and the greater Guayana region were the crown of El Dorado. Stern, however, was more interested in gold crystals, rare creations of nature that welded gold into strange shapes. "Only 1% of all gold are in the form of crystals and most of these are found in the Gran Sabana," Stern said. "And I have a fantastic collection that many envy."

Stern showed us a few exhibition catalogues, pointing to selected pages, "I sold them this. I found that. That was mine." He pointed to a framed poster with a blown-up shot of a gold crystal almost resembling

Alejandro Stern, the gold and diamond merchant, and his gun.

an exuberant grove of trees. "I sold that to a German dealer and now they are going to display them at the Cologne Gold Show." He pulled his drawer and pulled out a few small plastic bags of tiny golden-coloured bits and assorted clear crystals. He waved his magnifying glass over them and showed us the wonders of the world of gold crystals and diamonds. "I can give you a good price if you are interested."

Stern could sense we were not overly keen in gold shopping while on a natural expedition but was nonchalant about it. "Let me show you something more interesting," he smiled. He opened another drawer and took out a strange hard object the size of a bulky SLR camera. "This is a 5 million year old fossilised teeth of a giant shark. This whole region, the Amazon basin, was an inland sea and there were sharks here." He laughed and passed me the stone teeth.

"Show them your gun," Frank said. Stern laughed again and produced a respectable silver magnum from another drawer of his desk. "Santa Elena is a safe place, you know, but this business is a dangerous business. We have to be ready all the time" He placed the pistol on his desk, next to the plastic packs of gold crystals and diamonds.

"That would make a good picture," Frank said.

"Let me add some banknotes. That would be a better composition." Stern said, then roared with laughter. He walked over to a cabinet, took out a bundle of green 20 bolivars notes and placed them on the desk, too.

We snapped away with our cameras. "Hey Alejandro, show them the mafia chief in you." Frank suggested. Stern grinned and then held the gun in his hand, waving it. Salute the mafia chief!

***

We travelled on a 4WD through dirt roads to explore the areas west of Santa Elena. This is a godforsaken region between the savannah and the jungle parallel to the border with Brazil. There were the occasional Peman villages and a few military checkpoints to ensure no Brazilian crossed over to dig for gold but I doubt it would be effective given the remoteness and desolation of the place. We stopped at a gold dig run by a friend of Frank. These were poor men digging up the jungle in search for gold and other precious metals. They dig wherever they have discovered small black stones which could indicate gold but usually find nothing after digging out massive chunks of earth.

They live in primitive shacks and brave mosquitoes and diseases. It is a difficult life. The miner we met said he was very tired, having just dug a huge hole for nothing. Across the Amazon and adjoining wilderness, the poor and jobless try their luck in such places, destroying the environment in the process. Unless governments can provide viable job alternatives, there is nothing to stop them from destroying the green realm of Mother Earth.

We visited the village of El Pauji, which is famous for its artists, but were not impressed. Run-down, spread out and simplistic art pieces are made by hippies here. We visited a maker of incense who looked like a classic drug-crazed hippie who also offered lodging to backpackers who bothered to make the difficult journey here. Apart from making incense in a primitive way from some Amazonian plant, he also grew all sorts of crops to uphold an organic and green way of life. But everything was haphazard and on a small scale.

We had a tasty chicken rice meal at a hilltop restaurant near Pauji and then climbed Wakantepui overlooking the small stream between Venezuela and Brazil. The northern side was the Venezuelan savannah and the other the deep green tropical rain forests of the Brazilian Amazon. What a fantastic view!

We drove back to Santa Elena area, crossing the border into Brazil's Pacaraima town. There were no immigration controls for Pacaraima and Santa Elena. The only red tape was H1N1 health declaration forms to be filled up on the Brazilian side. We shopped at Pacaraima and had Brazilian grilled meat buffet, which was too dry for our liking. We also had some good Venezuelan wine that we bought earlier in Santa Elena.

***

We drove across the Gran Sabana with Frank. This endless expense of grassland, broken only by mysterious tepuis, reminded me of the borderless horizons of the Mongolian plains, Kazak steppes and Patagonian grasslands. What timeless beauty! The only pity was that the supposedly spectacular view of Mt Roraima, which lies on the border of Venezuela, Brazil and Guyana and the main subject of the novel, *The Lost World*, was unfortunately blocked by mist. We could only see a vague silhouette of this mountain. We also visited a number of waterfalls, the most unique of which was Jasper Falls. Red jasper stones, so magical and unreal, formed the bottom of the falls and the river that flew through it.

***

We left the Gran Sabana plateau to enter the tropical jungle lowlands of Guayana, adjacent to the independent English-speaking country of Guyana, 80% of whose territory is claimed by successive Venezuelan governments. This is the legendary land of El Dorado, i.e. 'the golden one'. An Indian legend spoke about an Indian chief who covered himself with gold dust and then dove into a lake of pure mountain

Across the Gran Sabana on a 4WD.

water, in a ritual that was the manifestation of the tribe's wealth and power. This legend had inspired many Spanish conquistadors to trek through difficult mountain and jungle terrain in Colombia and Venezuela in search of this legendary tribe and its king.

Today, a small town of El Dorado sits here where Venezuela's maximum-security prison is located. This region, together with the city of El Callao, is a major gold mining region. Venezuela produces 10% of the world's gold. We stopped by an unlicensed cottage mine here — one of the hundreds of impoverished, improvised mines in this region — just next to a state-owned one. We could get down 30 metres into the mine on a rope if we wanted to, but all three of us thought it was too dangerous. These miners, including a few pretty women, worked in teams. As with the miner we met near the Brazilian border, the work is tough and gold finds are rare and speculative, but the alternative would be hunger.

The jungle began to disappear and we saw more decent shops as we got closer to Ciudad Guayana. We reached Puerto Ordaz, the rich area of Ciudad Guayana, around 4pm. Fired by commodity prices and Asia's demand for steel and heavy metals, Ciudad Guayana is growing very fast. Frank said Ciudad Guayana is South America's fastest growing city.

Frank drove us around to see the dam that supplies electricity to Brazil, and the huge malls of the city. The city was full of condominiums and private bungalows. The Orinokin Mall is enormous — over 1km long! Lots of brand names here. This is a very American place like the richer suburbs of Caracas. Things were not cheap at the mall. Food was in fact quite expensive. About the food court prices in Singapore or more, and service was very slow. It took them half an hour to do my grilled chicken rice and it tasted horrible!

***

We flew 1,400km across this country twice the size of California to the student city of Merida in the High Andes, where people wear sweaters, speak in loud tones and mountain-bike to keep fit. From here, we did a foray to the Catatumbo region on sea-level Lake Maracaibo to experience the strange phenomena of daily lightning that seems to occur left, right and centre. The lightning of Catatumbo is an unusual natural phenomena caused by the meeting of cold air from the Andes and the hot air of the lake. Lightning would occur throughout the night despite the absence of thunder. Some scattered lightning started to occur around 9:30pm but the impressive phenomena really only took off around 11pm with multiple lightning blazing across the skies, some of which struck horizontally across. It was a pity that the night was cloudy and the lightning occurred all too fast, which meant it was difficult to take any photos without specialised equipment.

Back in Merida, we had dinner at a pizza restaurant where the bored chef got me to be the 'apprentice chef' and had Jayson film me making a full pizza, placing it into the oven and then taking it out to be cut. It was fun but I certainly messed up the pizza a bit and it was actually served to a paying customer, who did not seem too pleased about being a guinea pig to an amateur pizza chef! The Venezuelans sure like to have fun and play with their food! Obviously there is a cultural difference with some parts of the world where professionalism is prized over fun.

The boundless horizons of Gran Sabana.

***

I got onto an overnight bus to Coro, Falcon State, on the northwest coast of Venezuela. Coro was the first capital of Spanish Venezuela, before it was eventually moved to Caracas. Interestingly, it was also once the centre of a failed German attempt to establish a colony in South America. Its history has bestowed the city with a number of Spanish colonial buildings, many of which are well-preserved.

Today, Coro is an UNESCO World Heritage Site, although I have found its historical core zone rather small and many of the structures within the core have been modified for modern use. I visited a few of the churches and museums within the core colonial zone. The interior was somewhat barer than typical Latin churches, perhaps the result of many wars and conflicts in the past. The city is located in what is a rather dry coast with huge sand dunes in its northeast suburbs. Even then, it rained in the late afternoon, which turned the city streets into sudden streams of mini flash floods.

As I watched the rain from the safety of my hotel café, I wondered about this beautiful country, its fun-loving people, and the self-declared messiah that rules this nation. Would he bring Little Venice to the glories of 21st century socialism, or down the drain like the mud and rubbish flowing across the streets of this old city?

POSTSCRIPT:

Hugo Chavez's show is continuing. The Venezuelan economy is now entirely backed by oil prices, without which, as international critics contend, everything would fall apart. Venezuelan oil is also propping up Cuba, in exchange for Cuban medical doctors and advisors. Meanwhile, the homicide rate has climbed to 75 per 100,000 (from 49 four years ago)[1]. In Caracas, the rate is 220, which makes it the world's most violent city. In January 2010, Venezuela's power supply system came close to complete

---

[1] *The Economist*, 19 August 2010.

collapse, in the wake of a drought that lowered water levels behind the nation's largest hydroelectric dam to a record low. Critics blamed the government for under-investing in infrastructure while pursuing costly foreign policy and political projects.

The Gran Sabana

Jurassic landscapes: The Lost World of the tepuis. View from a small plane we flew from Canaima to Santa Elena. We survived three thunderstorms on this flight!

Picturesque Lake Canaima and the many waterfalls emptying into the lake.

Close-up of one of the great waterfalls in the Canaima region.

The boundless plains of the Gran Sabana around Santa Elena.

On the wild, wild tracks of Gran Sabana.

Leave your own monument in Gran Sabana.

Paraguay —
Rotting Away in Asunción
(2002)

"You going to Paraguay?" My Brazilian landlady asked me. "Be careful, the Paraguayans are strange people. They will eat you up," she giggled, as I walked out of the pension with my backpack.

Poor, deepest Paraguay: a landlocked country in the middle of the South American continent, the size of California but with only five million people. It is also one of the poorest countries in South America, with an underdeveloped infrastructure, so much so that Brazilians have told me that they feel like people from the First World when they visit Paraguay. None of their neighbours love them. The Brazilians accuse them of being thieves and smugglers, while the Argentineans bully Paraguayan guest workers. More than a hundred years ago, the Brazilians and Argentineans swallowed huge chunks of Paraguayan territory; the Bolivians tried a few decades later, but had their land taken by Paraguay instead.

Most tourists skip Paraguay. The country does not sell itself and its undeserved, unsavoury reputation often frightens the mildly adventurous ones.

The country's situation is not helped by the fact that the country requires visas from many non-European nationalities, which means that Australians and Singaporeans have to get a visa, and to get it, one has to furnish a statement from one's home police station stating the lack of a criminal conviction. Somehow, that does nothing to improve Paraguay's reputation as a haven for smugglers, drug-traffickers,

Nazi veterans, overthrown dictators, money launderers and assorted criminals.

Paraguay is definitely not just another boring banana republic. Its history is full of powerful personalities and events, some of which were motivated by worthy ideals, others by national and personal glories, although everything seems to have collapsed in disaster, sometimes through its own fault, and sometimes through the jealousy of greater powers.

***

I entered Paraguay from Brazil, at Ciudad del Este, formerly known as Ciudad Presidente Stroessner, after the long time dictator of the country. This city was a gigantic shopping centre for Brazilians who came for cheap electronic goods, perfume, drugs and women. An endless traffic jam greeted visitors, no different from those towns on the common borders of a rich country next to a poor one. I walked across the Friendship Bridge — beware of such names, they tend to imply the exact opposite, like the one between China and Vietnam, and Uzbekistan and Afghanistan — and got my passport stamped. Border security was next to non-existent. If one took a local bus, it went straight to the bus terminus in Ciudad del Este, which was a few kilometres away. Citizens of the neighbouring countries only required an ID to cross the frontier. Too many complacent tourists have forgotten to get their passports stamped and have gotten into trouble when leaving Paraguay.

Cuidad del Este was a dirty place. Rubbish everywhere, buildings unpainted, potholes on the streets and beggars stared at strangers in this messy strange place. Melon rind and seeds on the ground indicated the fruit of the season. As I walked along the sloping shopping street just outside the customs office, I suddenly realised that this was also a Chinatown of sorts — right in the heart of the South American jungle. Owing to the liberal taxation and immigration environment, as in the case of Foz do Iguacu, large numbers of Chinese and Taiwanese have settled here. I spent the next two hours entertained by a Chinese shopkeeper and his wife, with a never-ending flow of water, tea and watermelon.

"Why do you come here? There is nothing to see here. Such a rundown place," said old Zhang, previously a steel-worker from Tianjin. Tanned and roughened by the decaying heat of the humid tropics, old Zhang's face was testimony to the millions of working class mainland Chinese who have left their homes in the last two decades to seek fortunes in faraway lands. Economic reforms have led to the bankruptcy of numerous state-owned enterprises in China and these impoverished workers, previously the glamourised fighters of the working class, have been left to fend for themselves.

Old Zhang moved here eight years ago, when he was laid off by his factory after 15 years of service. He got onto a boat supposedly going to the United States, but it was abandoned in Peru. He was yet another victim of human traffickers and conmen. Stranded in this faraway continent, he made his way down south to a place he heard was easy to get in and where there was some money to be made. Here, at least he could make some money and send some back home. That would have been better than telling others of his supposed transit in the US. Face, after all, was still important in China; and so he worked hard, initially for another Chinese shopkeeper and then later began running his own shop.

There I was, in the heart of the South American jungle, having a Mandarin conversation in a shop full of oversized Shandong-made bras, tacky Fujian counterfeit Barbie dolls and suspicious-looking perfume of unknown origin, with business deals conducted in Brazilian reals, Paraguay guarani and the US dollar. Argentinean peso, once popular here, was no longer accepted. Twenty percent of the population in Ciudad del Este and most of its wealth were owned by Chinese and Taiwanese people who had moved into this easygoing land to run businesses, and perhaps to move into the US at a later date.

There was even a Chinese television station and, of course, a Chinese triad member who imposed a monopoly on, strangely enough, umbrellas and keeping everyone in line. No wonder some Chinese were very guarded about their background when I spoke to them in Foz do Iguacu. They might have wondered why I was curious about them. Another emerging triad perhaps?

Even without the triads, Ciudad del Este was a dangerous place — a large city in a poor country.

"You will be robbed on the main avenue if you stay out after dark. Get out before it gets too late — there's nothing to see anyway." Old Zhang gave me yet another slice of watermelon and threw the rind of the one he had just finished on the road outside his shop, adding to the already growing pile of rubbish in this dirty city.

Old Zhang called for a motor-taxi, paid the rider some guarani, the local currency named after the predominant Indian tongue, and off I went to the bus terminus, on a motorcycle in this weird town in the middle of nowhere.

***

The Pantheon of National Heroes in Asunción, Paraguay.

Flat, almost empty savannah plains interrupted by herds of cattle, isolated *estancias* (farms) and villages, and occasionally shops run by Asians — as indicated by signboards in Korean, Chinese and Japanese — in the middle of nowhere. Paraguay, like Brazil, had attracted immigrants from a number of countries that are today fairly well off. I came across Paraguayans of Japanese, Korean and German descent. Their children, without rosy cheeks in this tropical land, barefooted and in faded T-shirts, played with the locals in the playground; shops bore signboards that one would have expected to see in Osaka, Pusan or Munich. Many in the past had thought that this country was a land of opportunities. Today, their children might well be quietly blaming their parents for choosing the wrong country to move to.

***

Independence from Spain came to Paraguay in the 19th century. Dictator Gaspar R De Francia, 'El Supremo', imposed a policy of isolation and self-sufficiency. His successor, Carlos Antonio Lopez, began a process of modernisation which introduced one of the first railway lines and telegraph systems in South America. His son, Francisco Solano Lopez, continued the work and built a formidable army, one of the largest in South America. He saw himself as a South American Napoleon and got Paraguay to wage war against Brazil, Uruguay and Argentina in what was known as the War of the Triple Alliance. He died in battle, together with more than 70% of the population, including 95% of male Paraguayans. This had to be one of the greatest disasters in history and Paraguay never quite recovered from it.

Even today, however, Francia and the two Lopezs remain national heroes, their portraits appearing on banknotes and coins, and their bodies lying in the Pantheon of National Heroes in the City Centre, with a permanent guard of honour. The statue of Francisco Lopez on his leaping horse stands near the Presidential Palace, with the unfortunate irony of the entrance of a shantytown barely metres away. Paraguay continues to live in its past, for the present is perhaps unpalatable.

***

This is a very flat country, and yet it took me five hours to reach Asunción, capital of Paraguay, some 300km from Ciudad del Este. The road was not only full of potholes but our journey was made longer by countless police checkpoints: about once every half hour (for drugs, unpaid duties and perhaps random bribes). At a checkpoint in the middle of nowhere, 30 boxes of cigarettes were taken from the bus I was in. There, the police were also directing a crowd unloading thousands of boxes of untaxed underwear. Perhaps the police here were incorruptible. It was more likely to have been a showcase mission.

***

Asunción was a dead town on Sundays and only slightly better on weekday nights. It was one of those places that few tourists visited and few guidebooks cared to update. With my heavy backpack, I knocked on the doors of a few hotels — a glorified term for the ramshackle rundown shops — only to realise that some of them no longer existed or had been turned into love hotels. Finally, I decided to stay at a pension run by a fat shirtless Brazilian man, his second wife and their three teenage sons, and a daughter from the man's earlier marriage. It was not really an act of choice, but more a case of my feet telling me they could not take it anymore. This used to be a Korean-run hotel but it seemed to have degenerated into a rather dilapidated complex split up by ten or more households. Of course, I could have chosen Chaco, Guarani or any other 4-star setup, but beggars could not be choosers.

I covered the city in four hours: all the museums appeared to be closed, and for the rest of the week, too. A pity, or maybe the Paraguayans did not understand tourism. I spent the next few days surfing the net, rotting in cafes, buying tacky old postcards (such as one showing a local festival with a lady in national costume balancing five bottles on her head) and trying local dishes, for instance, the Sopa Paraguayo, which was actually a cake rather than a soup. After so many days in Asunción, I was even capable of guiding a few tourists who dropped by on what little there was to be seen.

Whatever it was, Paraguay continued to emit a decaying feel about things, amidst the humid tropical sun. When things rotted, they really smelled in such a climate. Not surprisingly, Paraguay was also the setting for Graham Greene's famous work, *The Honorary Consul*, where a young American doctor was involved in helping revolutionaries as well as having an affair with the wife of a diplomat.

Officially, Paraguay's chief exports are soybeans, cotton, cattle and hydro power, all of which are dependent on weather and the fortunes of its two large neighbours, Argentina and Brazil. However, what really drives this country is the money laundering, contraband and smuggling going on. These gave Paraguay a most unsavoury reputation and corrupted its bureaucracy and politicians, who are known to sell Paraguay passports to criminals and political exiles abroad, as well as giving refuge to fugitives and Nazis. The latest Transparency International Corruptions Perception Index lists Paraguay as the third most corrupted country in the world. Consider the amazing number of private jets at Asunción Airport. Would you want to invest in Paraguay? Perhaps an interesting place to do some private banking of the dodgy kind.

***

The yerba is the dried leaf of a shrub called *ilex paraguariensis* that grows in Paraguay and the surrounding regions of Brazil and Argentina. These leaves are roasted and then brewed in hollow gourds into a beverage called the *maté*. It is sucked into the mouth through a silver tube called the *bornbilla*. The *maté* is the national beverage of Paraguay, Argentina and Uruguay, and common in large parts of southern Brazil. The people in these regions drink a huge quantity of *maté* everyday, and anyone travelling in these regions would come across the typical local scene: a man leaning under the shade of a great tree, the *maté* gourd in his hand and indulging in his favourite mix of yerba *maté* through the *bornbilla*.

***

Argentina was burning. Three presidents in one week. I decided to skip Argentina, and head for Chile, although to reach Santiago from Asunción by land, I had to pass through Argentine territory. The problem was, the next available bus was in six days' time. I had no choice but to wait in hot, humid Paraguay.

***

I travelled 400km on a wacky country bus for six hours a few days earlier to the border city of Encarnacion, where I stayed overnight and caught another local bus to the old Jesuit settlement of Trinidad.

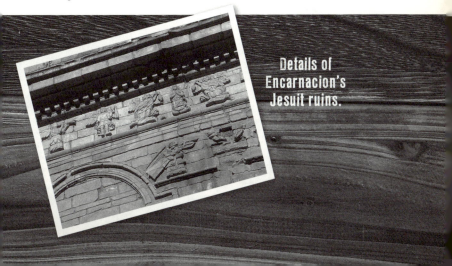

Details of Encarnacion's Jesuit ruins.

There it was, the remains of this grand experiment to liberate the Indians from the domination of the great imperial powers, tragically destroyed by the powers who did not want to see the rise of a successful Indian community. The only legacy of that episode was perhaps the integration of the Spanish immigrants with the Guarani Indians, whose language was the second national language of Paraguay.

I had *yakisoba* in a Japanese café in Encarnacion, its elderly owner disappointed that I could not speak Japanese, but nevertheless he switched on the television and onto a Japanese channel. That was life. The economic forecasts were wrong. Again, wrong emigration decisions.

***

Back at Asunción, the daughter of the pension's owner tried to seduce me. Maria, the *mestiso* beauty with mixed Portuguese-Brazilian and Guarani Indian parentage, entered my room suddenly without knocking and smiled gently with her large shiny eyes; she had the exotic look so typical of offsprings with a mixed racial heritage.

"Have a glass of *tereré*," as she handed me the icy cold version of *maté*. She sat herself on the sofa, in a rather tantalising pose a la Cleopatra.

"You remind me of my Korean boyfriend," said Maria, as she placed her hand on my thigh.

I sipped the *tereré*, which was a cooling relief in the 38°C heat. "Really? Thanks. I'm sure you miss him."

I would rather have taken a cold shower than engage in sticky passion in a rather dirty room with showers that did not function all that well. The cockroaches I saw roaming around in the room did not exactly inspire any sexual inclinations.

I returned the *tereré* to Maria and began rearranging my backpack. It was time to leave Paraguay.

POSTSCRIPT:

Paraguay continues to be an odd character in South America. In 2008, the country elected left-wing Fernando Lugo, a former bishop, as president. It was then subsequently reported that three women had accused the president of fathering their children while being a bishop. The president has since admitted to past indiscretions with one of them, and remains the head of state pending the resolution of the paternity suits.

The Amazon —
I Fed on Piranhas
and Mosquitoes Fed on Me
(2002)

I escaped from the cold, wet Peruvian Highlands into the arid, desert plains of the coast, before flying into the damp, humid jungles of the Amazon. Peru was an amazing country! The sheer diversity of landscapes, people and fauna was nothing short of spectacular. One moment I was complaining of the cold, rainy weather in places with altitudes averaging 3,000m above sea level and within days, I was on a plain that had not seen rainfall for a while. I had a wonderful time sandboarding and suntanning; and soon after, I found myself in hot tropical rainforests, battling heat and mosquitoes.

***

Can you imagine a city with half a million people in the deep jungle, unconnected to the outside world except by air and slow riverboat? Welcome to Iquitos, one of the largest cities in Peru, but it is more closely linked with other isolated communities in the hot humid basin of the Amazon, the world's most voluminous river.

I flew in on a TANS flight and immediately went on a three-day trip to the jungle, which was evidenced by the more than 40 mosquito bites on each arm, 30 on each leg and countless others on my shoulders. I suppose my blood was sweet, or the Amazonian mosquitoes would not have been crying out for more. I prayed that none of them carried the malaria virus, for although I had taken the

Yellow Fever vaccination, I did not have the patience for the ensuing two months of pre-visit intake of malaria pills. I saw mosquitoes 5cm in length, but thank goodness I did not meet those twice as large and found only in the deepest reaches of the jungle. The latter would not only bite you, but would also lay two dozen eggs into the wound. Just imagine watching the little maggots growing in your wound... what a wonderful pre-lunch tale!

Why did I pay so much to visit a jungle? Did I not have enough of mosquito bites during my army days?

***

Iquitos is a strange little place. A large city with a small town feel. It is part of Peru, yet located in the hot tropical jungle. A local told me that this was not Peru, it was the Amazon. No wonder the large military garrison there held a massive parade every Sunday to remind the locals who they were. I had just watched one from a balcony facing the central

View over the
Peruvian Amazon.

square, while having English tea in a restaurant run by the British Honorary Consul in the Iron House, an iron-plated building designed by Eiffel (who built the Eiffel Tower in Paris) a hundred years ago and shipped piece by piece up the Amazon to that particular town.

Those were the days of the Great Rubber Boom, which turned the town and others along the Amazon River (briefly) into the world's richest towns. Grand old mansions were built and professional opera performances travelled upriver to entertain the rubber barons. This lasted until the Rubber Boom shifted to British Malaya, after a sneaky British agent smuggled rubber seeds to Malaya. This event in history was somewhat related to me — it was one reason for the Chinese emigration that changed the demographic landscape of Malaysia and Singapore, and one of the reasons why my family ended up in Singapore.

Despite its remoteness, Iquitos has a large Chinese community and many Peruvians here have partial Chinese ancestry. Many have mixed Chinese, Indian and Peruvian blood. Many Chinese people moved here during the Great Rubber Boom to work on the plantations. After the bursting of the boom, with no funds to return to China, many of the Chinese settled here and married into the local Indian tribes.

I met many Peruvians who said that they had Chinese great-great grandfathers, including my jungle guide, Roberto Tang, who did not look Chinese at all — the result of being a fourth generation Chinese — with only 25% Chinese ethnicity but retaining a Chinese surname. He looked more Indian and Latino, although he said his grandfather was almost completely Chinese in looks. He said that there were some villages where Chinese people had settled down and interbred amongst themselves, resulting in everyone in those villages having Chinese features, although they all had Catholic first names (many had changed their surname to 'Flores' in order to facilitate naturalisation) and spoke only the Spanish and Indian languages! It was so strange to find our 'lost cousins' in the middle of the deep Amazon jungle.

***

The Amazon is the largest expanse of tropical rainforest in the world. It is often known as the Lungs of the World, as one-sixth of the Earth's oxygen originates here. It is also an area of diverse wildlife and plant-life. The continued destruction of this jungle and its wildlife threatens the survival of mankind, and the eco-diversity of this planet. Many areas along the river are crowded with farming villages, such that they no longer have as rich a wildlife as there used to be just a few decades ago. My guide remembered the days when any casual observer would see alligators and anacondas along the banks. These days, one has to trek into deeper jungle and tributaries just to see a few surviving ones. He jokingly reckoned that within ten years, he would be out of a job because there would be nothing left to see.

Even then, during those few days in the jungle, I did manage to see and learn about the amazing wildlife in these parts. Forget about the alligator and the pink dolphin. The former did not hold much of an attraction for me apart from the fact that they tasted quite good — tender and fatless, and quite a healthy meat, too! The pink dolphins looked cute but since they were protected, they were meaningless to a Chinese gourmet like me (just joking)!

Roberto Tang showing us a piranha he caught.

Do you remember the movie about the little fishes, the piranhas, that would attack young couples frolicking in the water, or jump out suddenly from the water to attack people who were passing by? Though small in size, these fishes were often shown attacking large animals and humans in packs, tearing apart much larger creatures in mere minutes. In real life, as our jungle guide assured us, they were much friendlier than portrayed. They only attacked if there was blood. We were asked if we wanted to swim with the piranhas. Interesting idea, but I did not fancy finding out from the fishes about any little cuts I may have had but was unaware of.

One must also mention another 'friendly' fish in the Amazon, the caneros. They are tiny creatures, some of which are not visible to the human eye and the largest at only 5cm long. They like human urine and would attempt to enter the human body in groups, either through cuts, ears or any human orifice. Once inside, they would do a wonderful job eating their victim inside out. Just imagine the feeling of having dozens of little fishes, some smaller than little bugs, eating one's flesh from within!

I tasted piranhas, grilled with some salt. They were tasteless and extremely bony. If they did not kill you when alive, they might just choke you to death instead! Not all fishes were man-eaters. Some were extremely tasty, for instance, the paiche, a fish often found in local restaurants. They could grow up to 2.5 metres and were fruit-eaters. They have caused some deaths, though, when local fishermen overturned their canoes and drowned while attempting to catch these gigantic fishes.

***

I woke up at 5:45am to go to an air force base near Iquitos, in a small six-seater sea-plane. The other passengers were Peruvian and Brazilian traders — there was an active border trade in this tri-nation area, some of it legal and benign, and a fair bit of it probably of a dubious nature. The Andean nations comprise some of the world's largest producers of narcotics.

I had thought the flight would involve a wonderful low altitude view of the Amazon jungle canopy. Instead, I got a free tropical sauna experience in a terribly small, confined space guaranteed to make most people go insane. By the end of the two-hour flight, I was completely wet with perspiration and terribly disoriented, and almost fell into the river as I got off the plane.

Fortunately, the Peruvian passport control was easy to manage and within minutes, I was on a canoe taxi crossing the Amazon. On the other side were the twin cities of Leticia and Tambatinga, the former being the capital of the Colombian department of Amazonia and the latter a Brazilian border town. Off the boat, I walked into Leticia unmolested — there was hardly any border control. Their relaxed attitude was amazing, especially as the narcotics-producing centres were not far away.

I walked around this small city and visited the local museum in half an hour. Really, there was just not much to see. There were a number of small hotels, catering mainly to Colombians from other parts of the country visiting the capital of their Amazonian territories and the jungle surrounding it, as well as the occasional foreign visitor

The Chief of an Indian village I visited.

passing through from Peru to Brazil or the other way around. There were also a surprising number of casinos and quite a number of souvenir shops relative to the number of tourists present.

There was just not much to do. I dropped by Tabatinga on the Brazilian side of the border. Again, there were no obvious border markings (and hardly any formality at all) but one realised that the border had been crossed when the language on signboards suddenly became Portuguese rather than Spanish. Tabatinga was even more of a cowboy town with fewer buildings. Everything was fairly run down this side of the border. I bought a US$50 ticket for a 10-hour speedboat journey back to Iquitos, Peru, in the morning. I would have to get up at 4am to cross over to the Brazilian side to take the 5am boat ride. I did not have much of a choice, though. I was definitely not about to take that two-hour sauna flight again!

Back in Leticia, I lazed by the poolside of the top hotel in town, Anconada (I was not staying there but just using the pool). The television in the bar was switched on and the locals were watching exciting live reports from the war front some 500km north. The week before, the Colombian government had declared the ceasefire with Marxist rebels over, and marched into rebel-controlled territory which was the size of Switzerland. The news showed government air strikes, fleeing refugees and government troops in action. Here in Leticia, people went about their daily activities and tourists from other parts of Colombia checked out tours to the jungle. It was difficult to imagine that this was a country that had been in a state of civil war for the past 40 years.

Trouble in Colombia and Slowboat on the Amazon (2002)

Shortly after I had sent off my last email in Leticia, parts of this Colombian city suddenly fell into a blackout. It was only later that I read online about the guerrilla attack by the Revolutionary Armed Forces of Colombia (FARC) on power pylons that had plunged southern Colombia into darkness.

As I walked onto the streets looking for an unaffected bar, swarms of heavily armed soldiers with machine guns and rocket launchers appeared on the streets, patrolling on foot or in army jeeps. Gamblers streamed out of casinos and shopkeepers hastily shut their shops even if they were not affected by the blackout. Was a guerrilla attack about to take place? Or was looting going on somewhere? I decided that the wisest thing to do was to return to the hotel. I did not intend to get caught in any crossfire or get shot at by soldiers for violation of any curfew that I might not have been aware of.

The night passed peacefully and I woke up at 3:45am to take a taxi to Tabatinga, Leticia's twin town on the Brazilian side of the border. I was supposed to take the 5am speedboat along the Amazon to Iquitos, Peru. The empty roads also meant that I reached Tabatinga in only ten minutes, not a wise thing in this supposedly rough town at such an ungodly hour.

A few dodgy characters hung around the dockside and I took refuge outside the quay-guardian's office. A native Indian family was sleeping there, with a pet mongrel dog lying beside a little boy. There were no mosquitoes but there were some strange beetle-like insects flying around. The Amazon might have been a spectacular river, but there was one thing I really did not like about it: there were too many strange insects and illnesses that could give one some really unpleasant experiences.

The boat set off at 5:30am, full of Peruvians on border trade or visiting relations across the border, which was not an entirely unusual thing. I met a number of people who had spent time in Manuas, Brazil, or Leticia, Colombia. The communities along the Amazon had more in common with one another than with their capitals far away across the Andes or along the Atlantic. The boat crossed to the other side of the river to get our passports stamped at the Peruvian checkpoint. There, the official asked for a tip, pleading poverty and hunger. I gave him only US$2, which embarrassed both of us, but caused no further problems.

Unlike the Colombian side, the village of Santa Rosa was not heavily militarised, although Iquitos itself was full of military camps and installations. It was easy to forget that South American countries had complex border disputes with one another. Every Peruvian I had met reminded me that Leticia was once Peruvian, becoming Colombian only after the war of 1933. Ecuador still had claims over the Amazon region of Peru, even though it signed the 1941 Treaty of Rio de Janeiro after its military defeat by Peru, in which it recognised the current borders with Peru. Both nations had three more short wars in the following decades, the last being in 1995.

The boat sped upstream against the strong currents of the muddy brown Amazon, its water already rising, as it was the start of the rainy season. By May, at the peak of the deluge, water levels in this region would rise by 15m or more. That was why many houses were built on stilts, or were simply floating premises. All the fields would be covered with water and the locals would have to travel around by canoe. At Iquitos, the river was 4km wide, but the entire region would become a vast inland sea by May. This was hardly surprising. One should not forget that the Amazon Basin was once a huge sea bay with an outlet on the Pacific coast. The rise of the Andes millions of years ago cut off the inlet and forced it to flow eastwards into the Atlantic. During the process, sea creatures like dolphins, stingrays and sardines that were trapped in the Amazon also became acclimatised to fresh water in an amazing process of transformation.

A short while after passing the marine checkpoint, the boat stopped in the middle of nowhere and a small canoe slipped by. The captain and his assistant greeted the two guys on the canoe, who transferred a number of carefully wrapped boxes onto the boat. "Contraband cigarettes," a fellow passenger whispered into my ear. The whole operation began and ended in just two minutes and the canoe slipped away just as suddenly as it had appeared. For the rest of the day, similar loading and uploading occurred at least twice at other spots along the river. Another facet of border life, I supposed.

About five hours into the journey, the engine died down suddenly. The captain and his assistant tried to restart it but failed, and they rowed the boat to the bank of the great river, where they spent the next two and half hours repairing it. Ugly black river vultures encircled our boat, while we were covered by clouds of mosquitoes like halos over the heads of saints. Huge butterflies the size of human

Quick shot of an Amazonian riverside town. I was more concerned about getting robbed on the boat and hence hardly took any photos on this boat ride.

palms flashed across the riverbanks in their bright yellow and orange slashes, and two pink Amazon dolphins swam close by, making a strange mocking cry at these miserable human intruders into their long-held habitat. Dragonflies the size of huge hummingbirds flew past, together with the occasional pair of bright green parrots.

The parrots reminded me of those John Simpson, the BBC correspondent, had said tasted bland and slithery. I did not imagine that I would have enjoyed them, but it would have been good to try them anyway. In his book *Strange Places, Questionable People*, Simpson also wrote about monkeys (likened to eating babies, with the gamey flavour of an old guinea fowl), tapirs (tasted like fatty venison), cayman (a kind of crocodile which were white and watery), peccary (a kind of jungle pig, described as pork-flavoured cardboard), tortoise (tasted like chamois leather) and intestinal worms from jungle tortoises (which he never tried). Simpson did not appear to have enjoyed the food he had eaten in the jungle. What a pity, as Woody Allen said, "Nature is one big restaurant." I only hope they do not all disappear...

Tree trunks floated down the river, together with debris like plastic water bottles and flips-flops. A few natives rowed past in their dugout canoes. These suntanned locals of the Yugua and Ticuna tribes were dressed in faded secondhand T-shirts (I spied 'The Incredible Hulk' and 'Oregon University' on them) and torn shorts. In the old days, these were great warriors who used their formidable blowpipes to kill neighbouring tribal enemies and invading white men, and made shrunken heads from their successful kills by cutting off the heads of slain enemies, removing the crushed bones from the neck while keeping the hair and skin intact, then boiled and treated them with soil, grass and magic potions until they were smaller than the size of a human palm. Nice things to hang on one's doorway. These days, the natives entertained the odd tourists, hunted occasionally and planted some jungle potatoes.

When I visited their villages a few days before on a jungle tour, they had quickly changed into traditional grass skirts and tribal headdresses. The women, who had scarcely anything on apart from G-strings, quickly put on bead necklaces made from seeds of jungle fruits, to cover their bare chests. In other words, the men dressed down and the women dressed up when outsiders visited. They then performed a dance and tried to sell us tacky souvenirs. Some backpackers called this visiting the human zoo. Well, they needed to make a living and would, hopefully, enhance their standard of living. From the sales they made, I figured they did quite well. We had all received something in return.

The passengers were getting impatient but most found ways of entertaining themselves. The only Asian on the boat, I stuck out like a sore thumb in the crowd. People speculated on my origins as most could not figure out where *Singapur* (Singapore in Spanish) was located, and what the heck was a *Singapureño*, who was neither a *Japonese* nor a *Coreaño*, was a kind of *Chino* but not from China. In the end, someone decided that I should be called Fujimori, the former ethnic Japanese Peruvian President, who had fled to Japan in 2001 after videotapes were found of his intelligence chief bribing the entire elite of Lima. "Fujimori, Fujimori, Fujimori", the little boy who sat behind me went on to shout for the next eight hours or so.

The boat was finally repaired; however, it was no longer a speedboat but a limping old nag. There were two occasions when it actually stopped and had to be restarted. Not an encouraging thing when the sky suddenly burst into a storm on the horizon and the sharpest, whitest lightning I had ever seen in my life flashed over the jungle canopy. The Great River was probably about 5km wide at this point — it was almost a lake — and the further half was drenched in a deluge of heavy rain while our half remained calm and blue. Bravo, Santa Maria!

We had expected to reach Iquitos at 5pm, but only reached the pier at 10pm. What a journey!

Colombia — Searching for the War in Party Town (2002)

Colombia is El Dorado, the land of legendary wealth. Here, semi-isolated Indian tribes living in the deep jungles had crafted great pieces of art in gold and emeralds, in such sophistication known only in great river valley civilisations such as Egypt, China and India. It was for such riches that the Spanish Conquistadors marched into the deep jungles and raped, killed, and enslaved these noble tribes. A new people was born from these rampages, and from the ruins of the ancient ramparts, glorious colonial cities like Bogota, Popayan and Cartagena rose from the ashes.

Attracted by the gold and riches of the New World, Sir Francis Drake and other buccaneers attacked these cities like afternoon flies, and legends of heroism, treachery and tragedy fill the pages of local chronicles. The patriots under Simon Bolivar fought for the freedom of the Americas in this mountainous land, only to see the new Republic of Gran Colombia broken up into the present day states of Venezuela, Colombia, Ecuador, Panama and Peru.

Peace never really came to Colombia in any lasting sense. The 30 years of conflict in the 19th century between the Liberals and the Conservatives in Colombia was highlighted in *One Hundred Years of Solitude*, the masterpiece of Gabriel Garcia Marquez, Colombia's winner of the Nobel Prize for Literature. The war lasted so long that midway through it, no one really knew what they were fighting for, especially when, at times, the Conservatives became more liberal than the Liberals. What remained was only misery, death and the oppression of the afternoon tropical heat.

Indeed, this parallels the country's current 40 years of insurgency by guerrilla groups such as the FARC and ELN (National Liberation Army), as well as the subversion of the drug cartels and rightist paramilitaries. In spite of it all, Colombia has remained the land of miracles, like Macondo in Gabriel Garcia Marquez's book, where gypsies came visiting on flying carpets.

For the past three decades, Colombia has managed to avoid the debt crisis and has historically achieved an annual growth rate of 5%, apart from the last two years of global slowdown. Colombia is a major exporter of oil, emeralds and platinum, and the second largest cut flower producer in the world. The nation produces world-class writers and artists. Its coffee, branded as Cafe de Colombia, is world famous and fills the atmosphere with its sweet, strong aroma. Even its women, the most beautiful under the sun, win beauty contests all over the world.

***

Santa Fe de Bogota, or Bogota in short, is the capital of Colombia. Futuristic skyscrapers and buildings (including a huge glass pyramid that some hate) dot the city, together with wide freeways and flyovers, plus enormous flashy shopping malls and glass-covered banking towers, all of which contrast sharply with the shantytowns just beyond the hills. My old friend, the handsome and suave Juan Camilo, my LBS classmate and central banker, hosted me with great hospitality. I stayed in his wonderful apartment, in a building overlooking the city and next to the mayor's own residence, with heavily armed guards; in case, I supposed, the guerrillas launched an attack. Now, would one call that the safest or most dangerous place in town?

***

Bogota is a temple of culture and the arts. Top class museums and idyllic Bohemian cafes lined La Candelaria, the historical centre. My visit had coincided with the biennial Ibero-American Theatre Festival, which also meant that lots of strange characters who called themselves performance artists ran around the city in weird costumes doing ridiculous things like carrying television sets on their heads, so as to amuse the local 'culture vultures'.

We relaxed in the trendy bars of Bogota, watching the most beautiful people in the world walking by to the tunes of Shakira, Colombia's superstar and world-class Latin sensation.

"That's a supermodel," Juan Camilo would point to a long-haired goddess as she walked past us, "That's another one." It certainly felt as if Colombia was the world's factory for beautiful women.

We visited the Gold Museum, with its spectacular golden crafts of the El Dorado tribes and the Donacion Botero, with exhibits from the collections of Fernando Botero, the world-famous Colombian artist who specialised in the portrayal of anything fat (or size-challenged, to be politically correct), such as a fat Mona Lisa, or a fat Velazquez. In a country of beautiful women, Botero had to show mankind humility and reality.

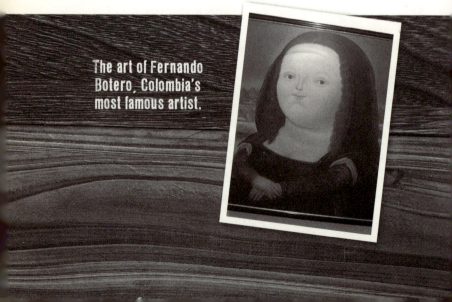

The art of Fernando Botero, Colombia's most famous artist.

I was introduced to Juan Camilo's friends and went clubbing in the party town's clubs, to the beats of Cumbias and Bambucos, dances of Colombia's Caribbean coast and Andean highlands. These people could really dance — I saw Juan Camilo transform from central banker to a flamboyant Latin gentleman. The vibrant movements combined with an element of graceful elegance projected a joyful and flamboyant spirit, with liberal doses of exoticism and eroticism — the legacy of a rich cultural heritage that reflects the origins of its peoples from Europe, Africa and the Americas. What could be more explosive than a mixture of the passions of Mediterranean Europe, Africa and the Caribbean?

***

Bogota is a fun city to live in. It is easy to forget that the surface prosperity masks a darker reality — the country is one of the largest producers of narcotics worldwide, and a bitter insurgency by half a dozen guerrilla groups has been going on for over 40 years, with 35,000 dead in the last ten years.

Public law and order is a major problem. The country is considered by many foreigners to be the most dangerous country in South America. The following are some statistics from John Young Pelton's *Dangerous Places*.

- Each day, at least ten people are killed in Bogata: 61 murders for every 100,000 people in any given year. During most years, more than 3,500 people are murdered in the capital.
- Colombia's overall murder rate of 81 per 1000,000 is nine times higher than the US average, placing it among the most violent countries in the world for murders. Others say it is only 53 per 1000,000.
- There are four kidnappings and 73 murders every day. A car is stolen every 24 minutes ad 142 houses are broken into every day.
- One pipeline near the Venezuelan border was blown-up 229 times during a 260-week period.

Across Colombia, soldiers guard towns and highways together with the right-wing paramilitaries grouped under the umbrella group United Self-Defence Forces of Colombia (AUC). At night, however, the soldiers retreat behind army camps while the countryside becomes the domain of the guerrillas, who operate in every department (or province) and threaten to bring the war into the cities. In response, the right-wing paramilitaries run rampant with the army closing an eye, vowing to eliminate anyone who cooperates with the guerrillas, but often accused of acting as the local mafia and death squad. More than 100 trade unionists have been murdered in 2002, along with the Archbishop of Cali in Colombia's third largest city, allegedly by such groups.

The future looks bleak and, indeed, this is the picture portrayed by the world media, but here in Bogota, the feel is that of a modern, prosperous party town. In fact, many travellers I spoke to felt safer here than in Sao Paulo, Mexico City or Caracas. Was I being too paranoid? Or was this the last burst of glory, like the glamorous balls of the British Raj on the eve of World War II, or like Gabriel Garcia Marquez's Macondo in *One Hundred Years of Solitude* during the great banana boom, just before the sudden deluge that destroyed its prosperity once and for all? In 2001, a US government report described the Colombian insurgency as the one that was most likely to succeed.

The impressive ramparts of Cartagena once stormed by Sir Francis Drake.

The world has since changed drastically. Since September 11, 2001, George W. Bush has been examining new options in respect of Colombia. A right-wing candidate whose father was killed by rebels was elected president in May 2002. The stakes are now higher than before.

***

After Bogota, I flew to Cartagena, Colombia's famous historic city and Caribbean resort in the north. Cartagena, Pearl of the Caribbean, has long been a city of legendary fame. It was here that the incredible riches of the New World were shipped to Europe. Pirates (or brave sailors of Her Majesty who were campaigning against the Spanish Empire, according to English history) and raiders like Sir Francis Drake and Henry Morgan had attacked the city countless times. The Spanish built beautiful mansions and palaces here, and guarded the city with massive ramparts and fortresses. The city was among the earliest to rise up against the Spaniards in the South American struggle for freedom and Simon Bolivar began one of his campaigns here. Today, the historic centre of Cartagena is protected by UNESCO as a World Heritage site.

After four days of high society living in Bogota, I traded Juan Camilo's fine apartment for a $7,000 per night room in Casa Vienna right in the heart of Getsemani, a colourful area traditionally inhabited by freed slaves, artisans and the commoners of old Cartagena. (The Colombian peso is also denoted as "$" and two thousand of these equate to a US dollar. Casa Vienna, with its US$3.50 rooms, is the definitive backpacker's den in Cartagena.) Here in Cartagena, the white, aristocratic and Andean feel of Bogota give way to the vibrant black and Caribbean rhythms of Cartagena, with all the colour and exotic quality of the tropics.

Cartagena and the northern coast of Colombia are the local equivalent of the Riviera. Tourism is big business there. Nice restaurants, bars and discos abound, and lots of young Colombian tourists from Bogota, Medellin and Cali, too, if one is looking for holiday romance. Not just on the beaches and in the old cities, but also in the famous Tayrona National Park near Santa Marta, renowned for its clear water ideal for diving, the amazing wildlife as well as pre-Columbian ruins. Tour operators and the local tourist office say that the national park is safe. Of course it is, as an interesting arrangement exists between the FARC rebels and the right-wing paramilitary, both of whom have camps within the national park to obtain a cut of the lucrative tourist trade.

When one joins a local tour to Tayrona, the payment enriches both sides of the conflict and enables the payer, along with the millions of tourists on the Colombian coast, to have a good time while battles rage not too far away. The Colombian groups, including the supposedly leftist guerrillas, have mastered the art of detachment and modern capitalist principles.

Unfortunately for me, this arrangement did not extend to Aracataca, hometown of the great Colombian writer, Gabriel Garcia Marquez (GGM). I had always wanted to visit Aracataca, which was supposedly GGM's inspiration for Macondo, the magical town founded by the Buendia family in his great work, *One Hundred Years of*

Solitude. Unfortunately, everyone told me not to go there because it was not just in the activity zone of one guerrilla group, but two — both the FARC and ELN were active there. The local commanders of these two groups did not get along well, so it was not just the possibility of clashes between the Army and the guerrillas, but also between the two guerrilla groups, that made the journey perilous.

***

Besides exploring the pretty old houses and narrow streets of Cartagena, I spent much time lazing around with the other nomads of Casa Vienna. In the mainstream media, Colombia is portrayed as a war zone and there are definitely fewer travellers here than anywhere else in South America. Those who travel to Colombia belong to a somewhat different breed. There are some who are more cautious, including myself, who would rather fly into and out of Colombia to avoid getting into trouble with roadblocks and guerrillas. There is another category of travellers who have no such fear. They travel round the country as though it is Disneyland and take great delight in whatever trouble they may land in. Quite a few have indeed come across guerrillas as well as the right-wing paramilitary, and a few have lost the odd camera and cash.

Here is a list of what to do if one's bus is stopped at a roadblock.

Find out who has stopped the bus. The situation would usually be fine if it is just the police or the army. Hopefully, passports and documents are at hand. Otherwise, a night in prison may be a fine reminder for future road trips around Colombia. Of course, one would be in for bigger trouble if drugs are found, or anything that betrays one's sympathy for the guerrillas. If that is indeed the case, have some cash and guts ready for tough bargaining.

If one is stopped by the FARC, ELN or any leftist guerrilla group, get ready to march off the bus with raised arms. They wear uniforms rather similar to the army, except that the FARC men have a bigger Colombian coat of arms on their shoulders. After marching off the bus, one would have to face the bus with arms raised, while the guerrillas search for weapons and documentation. Most of the time, there is no real danger, unless one works for a multinational corporation (MNC), the military, or the AUC (or similar right-wing paramilitary). If one works for an MNC, he or she will probably be kept as hostages for a big ransom, especially if one works for the big oil companies. They would also love you to bits, so do not worry — you are too valuable to them to let you come to any harm. If one belongs to the military, one may well face the possibility of being shot, but chances are that one would be held as a hostage for exchange of prisoners with the army. Good luck will be needed if one belongs to the right-wing paramilitary: he or she will probably be shot. It would be wise to learn one's prayers in advance, just in case. If one is just an ordinary tourist, he or she may sometimes be given a 'welcome to Colombia' greeting from the guerrillas. Sometimes, they will ask for a donation like Robin Hood, since the belief is that one must be wealthy to travel around. Of course, if one is American, he or she might be kept as a hostage on account of George W. Bush and his Plan Colombia efforts to crush the rebels and their lucrative drug

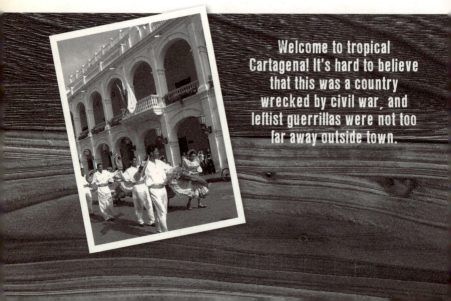

Welcome to tropical Cartagena! It's hard to believe that this was a country wrecked by civil war, and leftist guerrillas were not too far away outside town.

trade. One would probably be safe unless caught in a crossfire between the rebels and the military.

I have encountered a few travellers who have met the FARC in the countryside and managed to get away. One even had tea and a nice chat with them; but would people really want to try their luck with a group that has kidnapped and killed so many people?

If one is stopped by the right-wing paramilitary, get ready to lose money for many of them are plain robbers. They tend to be in civilian clothes, although some wear uniforms. It is the same routine: get ready to march off the bus with your arms raised behind your head. As a foreigner, one is probably safe apart from the potential loss of cash and camera. Keep them with you so that a friendlier AUC member might ask whether he could have your camera as a present. One may say 'no' and give him some cash instead, that is, if he decides not to take all your cash and camera as well. However, that would be better than leaving everything on the bus for them to take. Of course, some are not robbers, but even so, get ready to witness the rough handling of your fellow passengers and, in some cases, on-the-spot executions. Of course, these things do not happen all the time, but it is worth being mentally prepared. If one is found to be a left-wing sympathiser, as many NGO people are presumed by the right-wingers to be, pray really hard. Perhaps one should send an email to family members the day before any road trip so that they would know where to find your remains.

As you can see, it is really not that dangerous travelling around Colombia by road — that is, if you are prepared!

POSTSCRIPT:

President Uribe, who was elected in 2002, has recently retired after two terms in office. During his tenor, he had successfully cleared the leftist rebels from most of Colombia and demobilised most of the unruly right-wing paramilitary groups. He also signed free trade agreements with a number of countries and began reforms to reboot the long-stagnated economy. He left office with an impressive popularity rating of 76%. Colombia is now on the path to national recovery, although much remains to be done to entirely eradicate not only the FARC insurgency but also the rural poverty that sparked the rebellion in the first place.

EAST ASIA

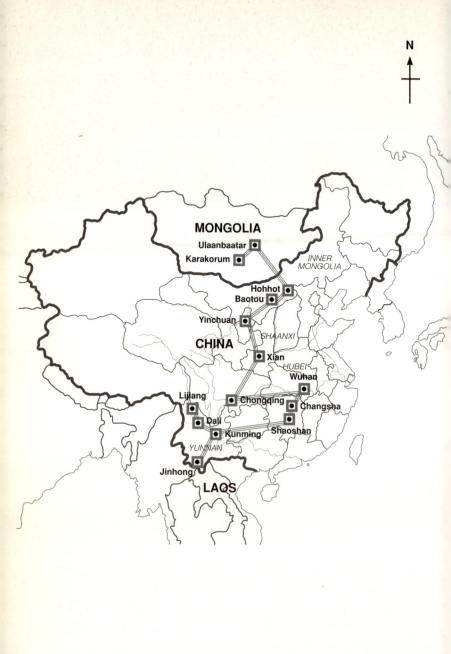

Mongolia — In Search of the Furry Mongolian Groundhog (2002)

"Autumn is the time for delicious *tarveg*," said Aldraa, the petite Mongolian girl with golden cheeks. Aldraa was the Mongolian colleague of Kenneth, my good friend in London and a fellow Singaporean who had temporarily traded his oil company executive suits for a six-month volunteer stint in Mongolia. *Tarveg* is the Mongol word for marmot, the furry groundhog found across the Mongolian plains.

Having tried numerous types of wildlife ranging from the Amazon tortoise to Greenlandic seal and Peruvian guinea pig in the past 12 months (perhaps politically incorrect to do so but certainly in accordance with time-honoured Asian tradition, while ensuring that none of it was illegal), I could not resist the temptation of the Mongolian marmot. So off we went in a jeep in search of this creature unknown to the Southeast Asian gastronomic adventurer.

***

Mongolia is one of the most sparsely populated nations in the world, with 2 million people living on 1.5 million km² of land. It is seemingly empty with endless steppes of rolling grass stretching all the way to the Ukraine, with shiny, brown hills and eternally snowcapped mountains, not to mention fine sands of the golden Gobi and deep green forests of the North.

The Mongols are a feared race in world history. They revolutionised cavalry warfare under the leadership of Genghis Khan (*Chinggis Khaan* or Universal King to the Mongols), who not only united the Mongol tribes but also turned the entire nation into a war machine. The Mongol *ger*, their white felt tent, quickly became the symbol of their armies of destruction. Nations that surrendered fast were treated with some benevolence, while those who resisted were wiped off the face of the Earth as examples for others. Countless great cities disappeared this way, from Baghdad (will a new Chinggis destroy the city yet again?) to Merv and Samarkand.

Under the banner of the blue wolf, the Mongols set up the greatest land empire in history, stretching from Hungary and Poland at the heart of Europe, to Korea at the eastern end of Asia; and from Lake Baikal in Siberia to the north, and to Java, Indonesia, to the south. The Mongol Khan saw himself as the King of the World and all lands not conquered by him were considered territories in a temporary state of rebellion. When the envoy of the King of France came for a visit, the Mongols demanded unpaid tributes and back taxes.

The Mongols reserved a particular contempt for the Chinese — Genghis Khan required his attendants to remind him daily that

the contemptible land of vegetable eaters remained on his southern borders. Only the meat eaters and free nomadic riders deserved to rule the world. Today, most rural Mongolians eat nothing but mutton and dairy products. Vegetables are still considered to be for wimps.

It was certainly easier to set up an empire on horseback than to govern one on it. The empire did not last more than a few generations and soon fell apart as rival princes struggled for land and loot. The efficient trading and postal network — the world's first common market and trade organisation of this scale — fell apart as warfare once again took over the land. The brutal subjugation of conquered lands eventually led to massive rebellions that destroyed the empire. Even Mongolia proper was eventually divided by its two powerful neighbours, Russia and China. Today, there are about seven million Mongols worldwide, four million in China, one million in Russia and only two million in Mongolia.

***

I arrived by train from Russia two weeks earlier. The friendly Mongolian border officials greeted me warmly. "Welcome to Mongolia," they said, as my passport was examined and stamped. This was in contrast to the rude, mono-lingual Russian officials who regarded tourists as an unnecessary hassle, perhaps even as unwelcome potential spies, terrorists and criminals who should not be allowed into the motherland in the first place. I felt liberated in Mongolia, no longer shouted at by police officers who interrogated and treated me as a potential criminal on a daily basis. Many of my fellow passengers had horror stories to tell. Some were accused of the most bizarre crimes and others had all their cash confiscated (running into US$3,000 in one particular case which I had heard about) merely because they had not been given customs declaration forms when they had first entered Russia.

Kenneth picked me up at the train station and before long we — together with Aldraa and Gana, our jeep driver — were out on the rolling plains of western Mongolia. Over the next few days, we were out in the hauntingly beautiful steppes of central Mongolia. We passed by countless *ovoos*, piles of stones set up at holy sites, together with offerings of vodka, cash and shreds of bright blue cloth — these were manifestations of the revival of Mongolia's ancient religion, shamanism. On the eve of the most auspicious day of the year, we witnessed a ceremony at a new *ovoo*, where lamas of Mongolia's Tibetan Buddhist faith chanted scriptures while shamans performed rites of offerings — in this timeless land, one could hardly tell whether a person was a Shamanist or Buddhist. Local faithful, mostly nomadic, herdsmen who had arrived on their horses and, yes, motorcycles, knelt in front of smaller *ovoos* surrounding the main one, each representing a different animal in the zodiac, under a full moon and cloudless sky. It was a magical moment.

We spent the night in a suspicious-looking hotel in the dusty, windswept village of Karakorum. Here, the inhabitants lived in wooden shacks and tin-roofed houses, with *gers* set up in their backyards. The memories of the free nomad persisted. Despite enforced

Karakorum, the ancient capital of the Mongols.

collectivisation and urbanisation by the communists, it had never disappeared, but had merely become a part of their modern reality. As democracy emerged after the collapse of the Soviet bloc, old traditions were reviving with a vengeance in this ancient land.

***

Daylight emerged quietly, creeping over the horizon like a late church-goer entering a church. I looked out of my window to find the rays of Apollo playing on the 108 white stupas of the Erdene Zuu Khiid, Mongolia's premier monastery. Did Nirvana lie beyond these magnificent walls?

Karakorum was the ancient capital of the Mongols, before Genghis Khan's grandson, Kublai Khan, moved the capital to Dadu (now known as Beijing) after the conquest of China — a move for which the Mongols never forgave him, as many Mongolians felt that it entrenched the influence of Chinese culture on many aspects of Mongolian life, from architecture to food.

In its heyday, Karakorum was a cosmopolitan city of great and small *gers*. Diplomats and traders — not just Marco Polo, who had been more interested in the prices of local women in his famous travel accounts — arrived from the far corners of the world, while priests and holy men of all religions competed for the souls of the Great Khan and his subjects. As the imperial fortunes collapsed, Karakorum suffered the fate that befell many of the Mongols' earlier victims. In 1388, the army of China's Ming Dynasty, which overthrew Mongol power in China, marched into Karakorum and destroyed the city in a way that left no stone unturned. Two hundred years after that, the great monastery of Erdene Zuu Khiid was built in its present location, over the ruins of the old capital. As prayer flags beat over the dusty plains, the fortress monastery and its white stupas stood out on the pastures like lonely witnesses to the ravages of history. I remembered the magnificent but sad facades of the mausoleum of

Sultan Sanjar at Merv, Turkmenistan, which I had visited less than two months earlier, the last remains of once-magnificent Merv, destroyed by the vengeful armies of the Mongols. How often history repeats itself. I watched the gathering duststorm in the west, and thought about the events unfolding along the Tigris. Historians call it the March of Folly.

We drove around the surrounding countryside, looking for obscure archaeological sites. The Orkhon Valley was the beloved homeland of the ancient Turks — the place from which their horsemen set off westwards across the plains of Eurasia and the Middle East, eventually reaching Anatolia and the Balkans, settling across the lands they passed through. Turks, Azeris, Turkmens, Kazaks, Kyrgyzs, Uzbeks and Ugyurs — these were all descendants of this great migration. Turks were fond of saying that one could speak Turkish from Sarajevo to the Great Wall of China. That might have been a slight exaggeration, but was not too far from the truth. What used to be the Turkic heartland has become the spiritual centre of the Mongolian nomads. Herdsmen roamed the wide valley and its plains, tending to their horses and sheep as they had done for the past millennium on these plains.

The hospitality of the Mongolian herdsmen was legendary. We stopped by several *gers* and were plied with sweets, yoghurt and more than desirable quantities of *airag* (fermented mare's milk) and *arkhi* (Mongolian vodka, also made from fermented mare's milk). The latter two are well known to travellers as products of acquired taste. Requests for short rides on their horses were greeted with great enthusiasm and we had a few brief moments of joy pretending to be members of the Great Khan's cavalry force.

Hearing about a wedding at a nearby *ger*, we invited ourselves there and were welcomed to join the party. We were treated as the most honoured guests and asked to sit together with the bride, bridegroom and their parents. As punishment for our intrusion, we were duly overwhelmed with large quantities of mutton soup, biscuits, sweets and seemingly endless cups of *airag* and *arkhi*. We were treated to an authentic

Mongolian concert as visiting guests sang traditional songs dedicated to the wedding couple, the herds, the land and all the good things of life. Sweet melodies prevailed in the increasingly crowded *ger*.

At this point, to my horror, I was asked to sing a song dedicated to the wedding couple. I had a sudden mental block. Besides, I had always thought that any exercise of my vocal cords would almost certainly crack glass windows (although there were none in the *ger*). So I decided to sing the nursery rhyme 'Mary had a Little Lamb', which was over almost as soon as I began.

"Tell them it's a song about sheep and goats," I told Aldraa.

That was received with enthusiastic applause and wide smiles. It was a subject the nomadic herdsmen could relate to. The guest from faraway Singapore cared about the local sheep and their masters. Welcome!

Gatecrashing a Mongolian wedding and enjoying local hospitality.

Welcome! Perhaps the only occasion in my life when I had ventured close to becoming a singing sensation!

We must have been the highlight of the wedding party, for we almost caused a minor riot when we wanted to leave. Everyone wanted to take pictures with us. Many of the guests rushed out of the *ger* to see us off, not to mention the other nearby herdsmen who had rode over because of the news of strange visitors at the local wedding. Even the bride and bridegroom came out to take a few snaps with us, together with their two-year-old child. The nomads moved in together whenever they liked each other and had children as and when they wanted to. Freedom was paramount to the nomads. Marriage certificates were for spineless urbanites oppressed by artificial rules and dubious notions of morality.

***

The two crazy Singaporeans and their equally mad Mongolian friends decided to conquer a steep hill rising above the plains. We charged up the hill in our battered jeep. What a wonderful view we had over this timeless land! The plains stretched as far as we could see. Men and horses were but tiny dots as the setting sun turned everything into a

Nomads on horses and bikes hunting for lost sheep.

shade of orange. What a beautiful scene. I felt myself falling in love with the land, something I had not quite expected as my journey entered its concluding phase. I wished the moment could have lasted forever.

***

Back at Ulaan Baatar (UB), I explored the local museums and relics of the ancient nomadic migrations across Eurasia, a topic which has long been my passion. At the local guesthouse, I met many interesting travellers and fellow techno nomads on the road, plus members of the local expatriate and NGO community whom Kenneth introduced to me. I also met two cool Singaporean sisters, Ming Lee and Ming Boon, and an intrepid English traveller, Emil. They were veterans of North Korea, Sikkim and other wild places. Between us, we must have covered more than half the world.

UB used to be a drab communist town transplanted from the Soviet planners' handbook onto the dusty plains of Mongolia. Nick Middleton once wrote a famous book, *Last Disco in Outer Mongolia*, about his journey in the 1980s when there was only one disco in this strange town, which stuck out like an alien spaceship on the great steppes. There were now countless discos, casinos, restaurants (including authentic Singapore and Thai restaurants) and bars in town. I visited the exuberant UB Palace, a gigantic disco complex, where revellers danced away like it would soon be the end of the world, no different from their counterparts elsewhere in the world.

***

We did not find the marmot. The dangers of the bubonic plague — commonly known as the Black Death, which wiped out a big portion of the European population during the Middle Ages — meant that fewer people were catching these creatures.

Marmot aside, I loved Mongolia. The temperature was dropping fast and I had to set off for the south. That night, I would be taking a 30-hour train journey to Hohhot ('Huhehaote' in Chinese), capital of the Chinese 'Autonomous Region' of Inner Mongolia.

POSTSCRIPT:

Mongolia remains an adventurers' destination, while the country is now experiencing a mining boom. Skyscrapers and luxury apartments, fired by an inflow of funds from mining groups overseas, are spurting overnight in Ulaan Baatar. Louis Vuitton opened a branch there this year and Mongolian luxury apartment developers have been seen at a road show in Singapore. Is this the beginning of a new era for Mongolia, or a mere Klondike of the season?

Across Inland China by Train (2002)

Did Genghis Khan Lose His Organs Here?

As my train rolled into Hohhot, I wondered if I had mistakenly boarded a train to Beijing or Shanghai. Here in Huhehaote (the Chinese name for Hohhot), capital of the Chinese province of Inner Mongolia (officially known as Nei Menggu Autonomous Region, although some may argue as to the amount of real autonomy it enjoyed), I was greeted by the sight of skyscrapers, gigantic shopping malls and zillions of bright shiny neon lights, advertising everything from mobile telephones to holidays in Southeast Asia (the latest craze among China's 150 million strong middle class was vacationing in what they called the 'Xin-Ma-Tai' travel route, referring to a standard tour of Singapore, Malaysia and Thailand). I had expected to arrive at a backward, dusty capital of one of China's poorest provinces. Instead, Timbuktu had turned into Las Vegas over the last decade during China's mad rush into development and economic prosperity.

Drastic changes have taken place in China in the 15 years since my first visit in 1987. Entering China again was most refreshing since my last visit was in 1997. No longer a poor, primitive and suspicious communist state, China has emerged as a confident progressive economic superpower with a huge middle class that aspired to and could afford the best things in life. It was certainly a capitalist and class-conscious society that still pretended to be classless and socialist in nature. While there is still a large poor rural population, a new middle-class has emerged.

The new economic prosperity was self-evident, even supposedly poor Inner Mongolia (poor in terms of provincial ranking in China) was ahead of Russia, where I had spent the preceding two months, in many ways. Well-dressed people, happy faces, well-stocked supermarkets and department stores with good quality goods at low prices, cheap and good food, plus variety to win your heart — and shop attendants who actually smiled and wanted to do business, taxis with meters, policemen who treated tourists with courtesy, and simple, plain law and order.

These were the things one would have expected in any normal country, but they were hardly present even in the most important Russian cities like Moscow or St Petersburg.

The Russians loved to complain that Chinese merchants had sold them low quality goods but the Chinese traders I have met have argued that the Russians could not afford the better quality items available in the department stores across China. This was a pity, as Russia began the 1990s on a stronger footing than China and the former was a country with a lot of well-educated people and a sophisticated level of technological development. Perhaps Putin would be able to make further advances.

***

Inner Mongolia, with its broad grasslands along the southern and eastern edges of independent Mongolia and a section straddling across an awkward bend of the Yellow River, was the 'Mother River' of Chinese civilisation. This, once known as Chahar and Suiyan, was also once the grazing ground for Genghis Khan's ferocious nomadic cavalry. Its fate became separate from that of central Mongolia (i.e. independent Mongolia) when its princes joined the Manchurians in the latter's conquest of China in the 17th century.

With the establishment of the Qing (or Manchu) Dynasty in China, the southern Mongolian princes of Chahar and Suiyan joined the new Manchurian Chinese Empire, with promises from the Manchus that their ancestral lands would be inviolable from Han Chinese settlement. They even joined the Manchus in the Manchu conquest of central Mongolia — why not? After all, they were marching against their historical enemies, the Khalka tribes in what is today Mongolia.

However, the Manchus did not keep to their bargain: when the pressure of peasant rebellions became too great in the 19th century, they opened Inner Mongolia to the landless Han farmers in China proper. Millions of farmers flooded across the great plains, in an exodus not too different from America's move to the West, or the Russian settlement of Siberia, during the same period — the guys I had met on the train from Ulaan Baatar to Hohhot were all fifth generation Han Chinese in Inner Mongolia. In 1911, when central Mongolia declared independence from China in the wake of the chaos that had engulfed China following the Republican Revolution (Tibet had also done the same thing at that time), Inner Mongolia's demographic landscape had already changed forever. Tsarist Russia and the new Republican Government of China agreed to allow 'temporary autonomy' (which, of course, became permanent) of central or 'Outer Mongolia', while keeping Inner Mongolia Chinese. After 1949, the communists accelerated settlement from other parts of China, but this was merely a continuation of a process that had already taken place well before they had come to power. Presently, only three million out of the 30 million inhabitants of Inner Mongolia are ethnic Mongols.

The cities of Inner Mongolia are no different today from those in other parts of China. There are, however, nominal symbols of its autonomous status, in particular, the use of bilingual signboards everywhere; i.e. Chinese and Mongolian, the latter in classical script, written vertically. Ironically, independent Mongolia uses the Cyrillic script, which was imposed by Stalin during the period of domination by the USSR, which began at her independence (only in name) until the collapse of the USSR in 1991.

The only other indication that Inner Mongolia was once linked to the independent Mongolian state were the names of businesses and brand names of local products, names such as Pastures, Genghis Khan, Mongol Khan, Horses and other symbols of the Mongolian plains that fired Chinese popular imagination. *Airag*, the Mongolian fermented mare's milk, and *arkhi*, the Mongolian milky vodka, which were available in Mongolia only from countryfolk selling them from barrels along the highways, have been beautifully packaged here in China with extravagant images of Mongolian herdsmen and iconology — Chinese style, that is. These fanciful products were aimed at a few free-spending Japanese tourists, as well as a vast, fast-growing number of domestic tourists from China's new middle class. They came here to see the pastures and pasture life. There were few *gers* (Mongolian tents, known as Menggu Bao in Chinese and *gers* in Mongolian) in the open plains here in Inner Mongolia, but tourist camps have been set up for these tourists. They are run like Chinese-style theme parks. Eleven in the morning was Mongolian wrestling time, 1pm Mongolian concert, 2pm archery and 3pm horse riding. Welcome to Inner Mongolia, China! Chinese commercial acumen has brought Mongolian culture into the world of Wal-Mart and Walt Disney.

***

Theme parks were not to my taste and so I did not visit any of them. I visited the Muslim quarter of Hohhot with its wonderful street food, and the Inner Mongolian Autonomous Region Museum with its interesting display of relics relating to the nomads of the Eurasian plains as well as ethnography of this region, which is not only inhabited by Hans and Mongols, but also a diverse range of desert and forest tribes, some of whom are related to other smallish Shamanist groups in Siberia. The museum was great, except that one had to get used to the ridiculous talk of class struggle (which was so ironical given China's current state of affairs — a capitalist dictatorship pretending to be communist) among the nomads and farmers of Inner Mongolia and pictures of happy, contented 'minority ethnic groups', who seemed more interested in dancing and singing.

Relations between the Han Chinese and other ethnic groups in China have often been mixed, rather than the happy images portrayed by the Chinese Communist Party (CCP) or the bloody, oppressive colonial type relationship featured in the Western media. There were exceptions, like Tibet and Xinjiang, where opposition was met with brutal oppression, but even then the reality was often very complex. China's incorporation of the border and ethnically diverse regions was hardly the friendly state of affairs as proclaimed by the CCP, nor in many cases pure military conquests regularly written about in Western accounts. Rather, it was more a confusing mixture of brutal military conquests, officially organised emigration of Han farmers, as well as unintended or even illegal emigration by landless farmers and refugees from wars and disasters, which the authorities did not anticipate and tolerate. It was a process that did not merely take place in the last five decades of communist rule but was a continuous trend over the past three millennia of chronicled Chinese history.

The southern Chinese are the result of the human mix between settlers and refugees from northern China, and the many diverse tribal groups which once inhabited southern China. The northern Chinese, on the other hand, are descendants of the original Chinese inhabitants of the Yellow Valley and the many assimilated invaders — mostly nomadic tribes from the Eurasian plains and Central Asia — who have conquered China many times in Chinese history. Unlike other conquerors elsewhere, those who conquered China tended to witness the demise of their own culture and their subsequent assimilation into Chinese culture. Even the ethnic Chinese communities in Southeast Asia were the result of this continuous process of emigration and assimilation.

Of course, if one had an entrenched preconception of something, everything seen would be perceived as proof of that theory. A Danish tourist I had met in Hohhot asked if the uniformed guy who spoke to me at the entrance of the local mosque was a PSB (a kind of political and public order police) who was trying to prevent foreigners from visiting 'oppressed minorities'. In reality, it had been a security officer who had merely informed me in a friendly fashion that I had to pay an entrance fee if I was not a Muslim. I am sure many tourists in China have also encountered such situations and have accepted it as yet another example of what they have read in the misinformed Western press. The reality is often more complex.

I went on to Dongsheng to visit Genghis Khan's Mausoleum. Genghis Khan's actual burial place was a secret — the Mongols were anxious that no one should disturb the graves of their leaders and all present at the funeral were slaughtered. However, the site of his death, where he died of fever after falling from a horse during his final expedition against the kingdom of Xixia, became a site of pilgrimage and annual ceremonies. Even after the fall of the Mongol-Yuan Dynasty of China, successive rulers of China — including the Ming and Qing dynasties, as well as the Kuomintang Republican regime and even the communists — gave official recognition and support to the founder of the Mongol Empire. A massive complex

Mausoleum of Genghis Khan in China's Inner Mongolia. But is this really where the Mongol leader was buried? Or is it a modern day political Disneyland?

stood at the site, with amazing frescoes on the life of Genghis Khan, complete with *gers* and a large *ovoo*.

A little known fact is that it was the Japanese invaders during World War II who first planned to build the mausoleum complex on the ceremonial site which, for hundreds of years, contained merely eight *gers*. They, too, wanted Mongolian support for their empire, but it was the communists who finally invested in the enormous present-day complex. I had lunch in a Mongolian restaurant at the site, and used the few Mongolian phrases I had learned in Ulaan Baatar. This earned me a free lunch as the Mongolian owners of the restaurant did not expect any foreigner or ethnic Chinese to speak even a few words of their language.

From Dongsheng, I hopped onto a pathetic classless bus to Yinchuan, capital of the Ningxia Hui Autonomous Region. The Hui people are actually Han Chinese Muslims, and many are also descendants of Arab traders who had settled in China and married the local Han Chinese over the past two millennia. They are different from the 9 million Ugyurs, who are Turkic Muslims living in Xinjiang. There are almost 20 million Hui in China, and they have been Muslims even before Islam reached Southeast Asia.

In the far outskirts of Yinchuan — again another mini Manhattan in what was one of China's poorest provinces — were the pyramidal mausoleums of the kings of Xixia. Xixia was a mysterious kingdom which once existed here a thousand years ago. This kingdom was founded by the Dangxiang tribe, which came from what was known as the border region of Tibet and Sichuan, but subsequently settled in this region as subjects of the Tang Dynasty.

During the Sung Dynasty, the chief of the now semi-Sinicised Dangxiang, who was also the local imperial governor, declared independence and founded the Xixia kingdom. The state lasted for 198 years, during which its arts and culture flourished (they created their own writing system, which borrowed some fundamental elements from the Chinese script, but with substantial modifications), together with some rather scandalous palace intrigue (for example, the founding king made his daughter-in-law his queen, and was then assassinated by his enraged son). The Xixia kings also built huge burial complexes, complete with pyramidal tombs. Eventually, the state was destroyed by the Mongols, but only after nine expeditions, of which Genghis Khan was involved in six.

It was during the last expedition that Genghis Khan fell from his horse and caught a fatal fever. On his deathbed, Genghis Khan decreed that his death should be kept a secret and whether or not Xixia surrendered peacefully, everybody in the kingdom was to be put to the sword. A month after his death, the Xixia king surrendered, not knowing that the great Khan had died and had left the most genocidal of instructions to his generals. The Xixia king was executed and all the cities and settlements of Xixia burnt and their inhabitants massacred. So much of Xixia culture was lost that even their script has not been fully understood today. I stood amongst the monumental pyramids of Xixia, desolate and lonely in the deserts of Ningxia and mourned for the dead, as I had done in August at the ruins of Merv in Turkmenistan, yet another legacy of Genghis's wrath.

There is, however, an alternative tale of Genghis Khan's death which I had read in Jasper Becker's *Lost Country: Mongolia Revealed.*

What remain of the pyramidal tombs of the Xixia emperors in what is today Ningxia Hui Autonomous Region in China.

This version claims that Genghis Khan craved for the Queen of Xixia and her legendary beauty, and had brought her to his imperial *ger* after capturing her. During the passionate session which followed, the humiliated queen suddenly brandished a hidden knife, severed the Khan's penis and killed herself. The Khan died from a loss of blood, rather than a fever resulting from a fall from his horse. So, which version would you prefer?

I hired a taxi to explore the remote monasteries and ancient archaeological sites of Ningxia's deserts and mountains. I climbed onto the crumbling mud-brick walls of the local stretch of the Great Wall. This was totally unrestored and untouched by tourists. To the north was the brown desert of the Gobi and to the south an unusual canyon with a surprisingly green valley in the midst of a dry plain. There was hardly a soul in this timeless corner of China. There, I heard the ghosts of warriors and adventurers of the past. Nations and tribes had come and gone. Empires had risen and fallen. Nothing was permanent.

Having had enough of Genghis Khan's exploits, I hopped onto a train for Xian and moved further south.

Buy a Mao Statue and Win the Lottery!

I took an overnight train across the dusty, yellowish loess plains that characterised much of the western part of China's Yellow River valley. The area in the present Shaanxi Province was the cradle of Chinese civilisation, hence the reference to the Yellow River as the Mother River of China. After two millennia of glory that ended with the collapse of the Tang Dynasty (the 'Renaissance of Chinese history') in 907AD, this region became a backwater area as the heart of the Chinese state moved southwards. Today, the Northwest of China (which officially includes the provinces of Shaanxi, Ningxia, Gansu, Qinghai and Xinjiang) is poor and backward compared to the coastal cities like Shanghai and Guangzhou.

Poor soil quality, desertification and poor transportation links to external markets have all compounded the problem. However, the Chinese government has offered investors tax breaks and incentives for investment in this vast region, in the hope that this long-forgotten region will catch up with the rest of the country. From appearances at least, there is new prosperity in the form of flashy new buildings and shopping malls. Many of the region's migrant workers have also returned after a stint in the industrial powerhouse of coastal China and, armed with new industrial know-how, have started to set up companies in their homeland. Perhaps this will bring vast changes to this region.

For the time being, the Northwest is still more closely related to the movies of Zhang Yimou, the award-winning Chinese director extraordinaire. Many of his movies, in particular, *Red Sorghum*, *Ju Dou* and *Raise the Red Lantern* were set in this region, where feudal traditions and poverty have long persisted. The desolation, as well as the empty, bleak landscape, has long attracted moviemakers as well as photographers looking for the unusual.

***

Xian, the capital of Shaanxi Province, was my destination. This city had the distinction of having been China's first imperial capital and also for being a capital for the longest period, in fact — one whole millennium. Beijing, made capital only under the Mongols in the 13th century, was a baby compared to Xian. It was in the destroyed city of Xianyang near Xian, that Qin Shihuangdi, China's first emperor, unifier and builder of the Great Wall, built his capital more than 2,200 years ago. It was also near this vicinity that he rested under a gigantic yet-to-be-excavated man-made hill, guarded by an entire army of 6,000 life-size terracotta warriors, horses and chariots. The latter was discovered in 1974 in what was one of the 20th century's greatest archaeological discoveries, ranking alongside King Tutankhamen's treasures in Egypt and Machu Picchu in Peru.

It was an amazing sight, to view these fully armed (with real, sharp swords and archery) warriors, every one with a different posture and facial expression. Qin Shihuangdi was an extraordinary ruler. He had come into power while still a teenager, manoeuvred through palace intrigue, united all of China and then ruled and reformed the country ruthlessly. Countless died in his grand projects (like the Great Wall) and numerous purges were made against dissidents and scholars. China's history is full of tyrants like him, many of whom were regarded as great rulers due to their achievements but also feared or loathed for their tyranny. It is this, as well as the continuing influence of the past, that makes Chinese history at once both controversial and interesting.

Xian, the former Chang-an ('Eternal Peace', as it was then known), was also the capital of the Tang Dynasty (618–907AD), the most glorious dynasty in Chinese history. Poets and writers have waxed lyrical about this cosmopolitan city, the eastern terminus of the Silk Road, where Arab and Central Asian traders dropped by with their exotic wares and goods, and brought highly-valued Chinese silk to the Middle East and Europe. Persian music was the fashion of the day and Tang ladies impressed their men with the latest Central Asian Turkic dances. Japanese and Korean scholars came to study Chinese

The loess landscapes of the Upper Yellow Valley in Ningxia.

The impressive walls of Xian and the Terracotta Warriors of China's First Emperor.

The Grand Mosque of China: China has 20 million Muslims.

statecraft and Buddhist philosophy. Today, the Japanese Imperial Court is the sole practitioner of Tang court protocol long lost in China, and Kyoto, Japan's old capital, is a textbook model of Tang city planning, and perhaps what old Chang-an once looked like.

Some Chinese like to talk about the concept of racial purity, ignoring the fact that the Tang Dynasty was prosperous because it was cosmopolitan. The later Ming Dynasty went into decline because it banned trade and cultural exchange, and forbade the Chinese from travelling abroad and foreigners from coming to China. One can easily see how London and New York have became global cities, and appreciate our leaders' efforts to entice more foreigners to Singapore. Having said that, empty local stomachs would still have to be fed. After all, the Tang Dynasty collapsed when peasants went hungry and rebellions sprouted like mushrooms. Cool cosmopolitanism alone would not have helped in such circumstances.

***

I visited the Grand Mosque of Xian, the largest in China, built by Arab traders and settlers during the Tang Dynasty. It has become the centre of Xian's Hui community. The Hui are Chinese Muslims, the product of that great era of international trade and coexistence in Xian. The mosque was built in a traditional Chinese style, i.e. with no difference from the architecture of Buddhist or Taoist temples, except that one would find the Islamic crescent on the traditional Chinese rooftop, complete with dragons and mythological creatures. Islam in China has blended in well with Chinese traditions and culture, and has adopted all forms of Chinese life except for obvious differences like the prohibition on consumption of pork and alcohol. Therefore, it should not be a surprise that the mosques were built like Chinese Buddhist or Taoist temples.

However, across China, in the mad rush for modernisation, many of these traditional Chinese-style mosques have been torn down and replaced with tall complexes with Arabesque domes. Some are ugly glass towers simply topped with a dome, a feature not associated with local traditions. I asked a Muslim official and was told that they, too, like the rest of China, want to be 'internationalist'. This is a pity. They have lost their heritage along the way. I hope they realise the mistake before it is too late.

The present Xian, despite its numerous monuments and cultural artefacts, is not a city loved by many visitors. It is terribly polluted. The heavy smog irritated me and I could hardly breathe. I wanted to get out as soon as I had visited the Terracotta Warriors. So, I hopped onto an overnight train to Chongqing.

***

Chongqing Municipality, China's newest provincial level administrative unit with 30 million people, is the largest city in southwest China. I was last here in 1995 on business. It is a huge industrial centre with heavy pollution. Chongqing, like most of China's cities, is full of skyscrapers. The rapid economic progress has changed China beyond recognition. Even locals tell me that they can hardly keep pace with the changes. Taxi drivers hardly know the new highways.

On my 1995 visit, I embarked on a six-hour drive through awful, potholed country roads to Dazu, a UNESCO-listed Buddhist grotto complex. The locals told me that the journey is now a smooth two-hour drive on the motorway. The standard of living has improved for most Chinese people, and they are travelling in vast numbers within their country and many have also travelled abroad for the first time. Ugly Stalinist-style buildings are being replaced with flashy new apartments, office blocks and shopping malls. However, old charming historic districts are also being bulldozed in this mad rush to modernise. A tragedy, for they may well turn all Chinese cities into soulless, American-style metropolises.

I got on a boat which was heading down the Yangtze River

(Changjiang in Chinese, meaning the 'Long River'), through the renowned Three Gorges (Sanxia). For a few millennia, the Sanxia, with its high cliffs and fjord-like scenery, has fascinated many Chinese travelling from the central plains to Sichuan, China's most populous province which is totally separated from the rest of China by tall mountains. Poets have sung about its beauty and famous painters made the difficult journey here to immortalise the gorges in their work. Today, hundreds of cruise boats do the journey for modern-day tourists and travellers, all for some cash and a sense of romanticism.

Sanxia has entered world headlines in the last decade. The Chinese government had decided to build the world's largest hydroelectric project by damming the Changjiang, and thereby submerging some of this spectacular scenery under water forever (although new scenic spots would appear) and forming one of the world's largest man-made lakes. Millions of people, including whole cities, would have to be relocated in the process. The Chinese argue that the project would help to control floods and generate electricity for China's fossil-poor inland provinces. Critics complain about the millions of people to be relocated and the damage to the ecological environment as well as archaeological sites along the river.

Chongqing on the Yangtze, where I got onto the Three Gorges cruise. This is officially the world's most populous municipality with over 30 million inhabitants.

I dropped by the city of Fengdu, which literally means 'Ghost City'. This was an old Chinese city with a hill full of temples and monuments relating to the Taoist-Buddhist vision of the underworld. To me, it was an ancient Disneyland of sorts, given that there were hardly any monks around and there were lots of souvenir stalls and money-grabbing schemes around (e.g. knock the bell for one yuan and that will bring good fortune). The dam project would completely submerge the city under the great lake to be formed.

I witnessed Fengdu's citizens moving out of their houses and workmen demolishing entire sections of the city already vacated. A new Fengdu was being built on the opposite bank of the river, on higher ground, in that all-so-prevalent Manhattan skyscraper style, which to the Chinese represented 'Progress' with a capital 'P'. The old Fengdu was literally becoming a ghost city.

We got on a smaller boat to explore the Wushan area and its shallow, narrow gorges, just off the Changjiang. This was one of China's poorest regions. Local children dressed in only underwear waded in the cold running water, stretching out long poles with a net at the end to tourist boats, begging for money. The China of today is a country with a huge regional income disparity. Anyone travelling in China would notice the vast number of domestic tourists — they tend to outnumber foreigners by 10 times or more — and they usually come from the prosperous eastern or coastal provinces of Guangdong or Zhejiang, or cities like Shanghai and Beijing, where incomes may well be more than 10 times higher than the poorest regions in the country. My boat was full of well-dressed Guangdong tourists with their expensive cameras and telescopes, throwing stacks of banknotes into the nets of these poor local children and snapping away at this heart-breaking scene with their digital cameras and videocams. They could well be Western tourists in Mozambique.

***

I stepped off the boat at Yichang and then onto a bus on yet another new motorway to Wuhan, capital of Hubei Province. Wuhan, right in the middle of China proper (i.e. minus the western minority ethnic areas), is another metropolis with 10 million people. This is the midpoint of the rail and river traffic from Chongqing in the west to Shanghai in the east, and also from Beijing in the north to Guangzhou in the south. A very strategic city that once hosted several international concessions.

The China of the 19th and early-20th century was a weak dying nation. As a result of several wars with Western powers, it was forced to grant parts (known as 'concessions') of over 30 cities to the Great Powers, where the Chinese had no police or administrative powers or the right to levy customs duties or taxes. Wuhan, Shanghai, Tianjin and numerous other cities were all concession cities. Such humiliating loss of sovereignty was among the many reasons which eventually led to the outbreak of the Xinhai Revolution in Wuhan which overthrew the Qing (or Manchu) Dynasty. The Chinese Republic was proclaimed, but it took decades before peace returned to the nation.

***

Changsha in Hunan Province was next on my journey. Welcome to the Land of Hot and Fiery Pepper! The Hunanese put chilli and pepper into everything they ate. Descendants of the exotic ethnic mix which comprised Han settlers who arrived 2,000 years ago with Qin Shihuangdi's army, and intermarriage with the local Tujia, Miao and Xiang tribes, the Hunanese have produced some of China's greatest rebels and political activists.

The most famous Hunanese is Mao Zedong, the founder of Communist China. The son of a modestly wealthy farmer, Mao became China's Communist master after decades of a bitter civil war. It was easier to build an empire than to govern one. Mao had made himself China's hero by getting rid of the ancient regime and its corrupt, feudal landlords and warlords, as well as the humiliating international concessions.

However, the new emperor was also a power grabber, control freak and an economic disaster case. He started the Cultural Revolution and other purges to get rid of potential rivals, thus condemning China's most talented to internal exile and personal ruin. His dubious notions of economic theories led to great famines and destruction of the nation's industrial capabilities, resulting in death for over 30 million people. His disregard of the nation's rich cultural heritage destroyed numerous historical and cultural relics.

It was only through Deng Xiaoping's reforms after Mao's death that China recovered from that era of destruction, desolation and international isolation. Capitalist style reforms, officially known as 'Socialism with Chinese Characteristics', have brought unknown prosperity to the country.

As the Communist Party prepared for its 16th congress, huge billboards proclaimed President Jiang's new 'ideological theories', the so-called 'Three Represents', which basically urged the party to represent the broadest groups of people in the country, and admit into the party hierarchy classes which communists have traditionally seen as enemies, the so-called 'patriotic entrepreneurs' (known to the rest of the world as capitalist businessmen), 'productive forces', and anyone who was not defined in traditional Marxist theories as peasant, worker or soldier. Basically, no more party of the proletariat but party of business and the nouveau riche. How times have changed. Sounds like the 'New Labour' movement in the UK.

A typical Westerner would regard Mao as a villain of the worst kind, the Chinese equivalent of Hitler and Stalin. However, most Chinese have mixed feelings about him. In Mao, they had the unfortunate combination of George Washington and Vladimir Lenin. They are aware of the terrible abuses and poverty during the Mao era, but his overthrow of the corrupt old feudal order in which China was a semi-colony of the Great Powers had placed him among the pantheon of great Chinese heroes, like Qin Shihuangdi (the first emperor and unifier of China) and Zhu Yuanzhang (liberator of China from Mongol rule and the tyrannical founder of the Ming Dynasty; also founder of the first Chinese secret police). Many are also nostalgic for the old days when everybody had a job and a similar standard of living (i.e. all were equally poor), and corruption (so prevalent in today's unofficially capitalist China) was almost nonexistent (or at least not obvious).

As I visited his home museum in nearby Shaoshan, together with thousands of local tourists, the museum guide shouted out with her loudspeaker, "Visit Chairman Mao's Home, Learn from Mao Thoughts and Help to Turn China Modern!" I nearly laughed aloud at the obvious irony of it all. Was it not Maoism that devastated China economically? Was it not capitalism, albeit practised with a vengeance in this officially communist state, that has turned China into the new emerging economic superpower?

Shaoshan's residents, mostly farmers, make much more hawking Mao souvenirs. They mob tourists with Mao caps, Mao statues, Mao CDs, Mao videos, Mao mouse pads and even Mao cuisine (e.g. try Mao's favourite dishes in the countless Mao cafes and restaurants in Shaoshan). In the eyes of the peasant and ordinary worker, especially

Visit the Mao-themed park at his hometown in Shaoshan.

in Hunan Province, Mao has become a kind of god. Here in Hunan, houses have Mao statues on their rooftops (instead of the typical dragon or bull symbolising good luck and prosperity), saying that these would frighten away demons and evil spirits. Taxi drivers have Mao talismans just above their steering wheels, also said to bring good luck. Touts tried to sell me Mao statues: "This would help you win the lottery," they said. From communist ruler to pop icon — Mao must be turning in his grave!

Legendary Taoist Doctor of the Jade Dragon Snow Mountain

The gentle autumn winds blowing across the foothills of the snowcapped Jade Dragon Snow Mountain and Naxi women working in the fields in their bluish costumes all add an unusually surreal atmosphere to Baisha ('White Sands' in Chinese), a remote village in northwestern Yunnan. Suddenly, the serenity of the scene was interrupted by an old man with a goatee dressed in white medical gown and cap.

"I am the famous Dr. Ho," he said. Oh yes, the famous Dr. Ho a la Bruce Chatwin. Bruce Chatwin, one of the greatest travel writers of the 20th century, first wrote about Dr. Ho in *The Times*, calling him "the legendary Taoist Doctor of the Jade Dragon Snow Mountain", whatever that implied. Dr. Ho was a medical doctor and there was nothing Taoist about him. Whatever it was, Chatwin's article had turned Dr. Ho into one of the most unusual characters lurking around this corner of China. Dr. Ho had become the regional celebrity, resulting in a stream of famous people (as well as non-entities like myself) dropping by his house in Baisha. This sudden bout of celebrity status had somehow gone to Dr. Ho's head, and he spent most of his time making his presence known to every foreign visitor to Baisha.

"Come in, come in," Dr. Ho said, "You must have heard of me. I am in every English guidebook, French one and Dutch, too. *Lonely Planet, Rough Guides...*" and on he went.

Tim, an American backpacker, and I stepped into his clinic. It looked more like a personal hall of fame rather than a rural clinic, with hundreds of news clippings (including his photographs) from newspapers worldwide, as well as thousands of name cards. It was interesting to note that most of the articles testified to his notoriety, rather than his skill in treating patients. In fact, *Lonely Planet* warned about his dodgy tea and the fact that guests were often asked to pay "what the tea is worth".

Dr. Ho handed us files that contained articles and assorted letters regarding his fame, and then poured us tea, what he called "my famous herbal tea". John Cleese, a British actor, was said to have remarked, "Interesting bloke, crap tea".

"Look at this letter," he pointed to one with faded ink, dog ears and tea stains, an indication of the number of hands it had been in. "This Swiss man was cured of cancer after drinking my tea," he said. "That hospital asked me about my miracle cure, yes, another proof of my skill."

Dr. Ho, the legendary Taoist doctor whom Bruce Chatwin met a few decades ago.

"This American's tumour had completely disappeared," he pointed to another letter, "but he didn't give me any money. That's fine, because I am happy so long as people are cured of their sickness."

"Have more," he said, as he poured more tea into our cups. I wondered how much I should pay him later.

Then he thrust a visitor's book at me, "This book is for Singapore visitors. See, many of you guys have come here." Then he passed a much thicker one to Tim, "Many Americans were here too, and all of them love me."

He walked around his room, saying, "Take your time, look at all the articles. See how famous I am."

I was curious about Bruce Chatwin and asked about him.

"Yes, I remember him. He came and we chatted about my work. Then he wrote about me. He died a few years ago." He seemed a little reluctant to talk about the very man who made him famous. The way he put it sounded as though Chatwin had died only recently. In fact, Chatwin died in 1989. I wondered if he was embarrassed that his fame was more due to a well-known writer's licence rather than his own medical credentials.

Tim was more concerned about his temperature and got a pack of herbal powder from him. "You will be OK in no time," Dr. Ho said. Tim gave him 20 yuan, which was less than US$3.

Then he passed us more documents and articles, as if we did not have enough of it.

"Thanks, Dr. Ho, we have to make our way to the Fairy's Peak Temple," I said.

"Yes, OK, thank you for visiting. Remember, when you get back, tell more people about me," he said.

So we succeeded in escaping from the infamous Dr. Ho. I am not sure what to make of this colourful character. Perhaps he was just a lonely person who craved attention. The Jade Dragon Snow Mountain might have been beautiful and living there may sound idyllic, but life there could also be boring even for an old man, and the visit from a writer more than a quarter of a century ago had created an unusual character in this remote part of the world. In a strange way, Bruce Chatwin continues to live here. If you happen to be a Bruce Chatwin fan, consider visiting his creation in Baisha, the pretty hamlet in the foothills of the Jade Dragon Snow Mountain.

***

Yunnan is one of China's southern-most provinces and perhaps the most diverse one in terms of geographical landscapes and ethnic makeup. During the previous few weeks, I had visited snowcapped mountains soaring up to over 4,000m above sea level, as well as hot and humid tropical rainforests. Yunnan is home to over 26 ethnic groups (close to half of China's 56), including a group of 13,000 Mongols who are descendants of Kublai Khan's army, trapped here since the collapse of the Mongol Empire in the 13th century. They have since become fishermen, perhaps the only solitary group of Mongolian fishermen in the world.

These ethnic groups account for about one-third of the province's population. If one visited the French supermarket chain

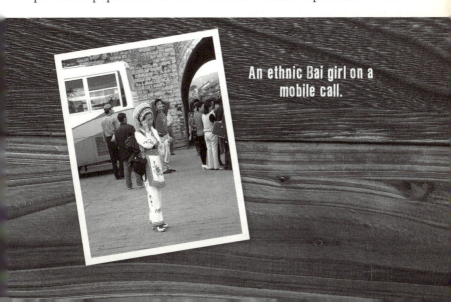

An ethnic Bai girl on a mobile call.

Carrefour's Kunming store, one would find traditional clothing from some of Yunnan's many ethnic and tribal groups. Maybe I should have checked out Wal-Mart and Parson's Kunming stores, too.

Yunnan is very popular with international backpackers. *Lonely Planet* says that if one had to choose one province to visit in China, it should be Yunnan. In spite of this and its similar popularity among domestic tourists, the province has retained its unique charm and its diverse ethnic groups have also done much to benefit from this boom in tourism.

I arrived in Kunming, the capital of Yunnan, from rainy Changsha. I fell in love immediately with this province and its clear blue sky. Eco-tourism was the catch phrase here, and one could even find different bins for biodegradable rubbish and non-degradable ones. Although most locals still dump their rubbish in the wrong places, having the right messages loudly promoted was a good start. Five years ago, nobody in China would have talked about environmental protection. Now, most were at least paying lip service to it (for example, many products in Chinese supermarkets carry labels calling themselves 'green products', and numerous public banners and billboards call for environmental protection), and some have realised its benefits and have started taking it seriously.

***

I took a five-hour bus journey — a decade ago the journey would have taken more than 20 hours — to Dali, a city in northwestern Yunnan, located on the shores of a lake called Er-hai, or the 'Sea of Er'. People who live deep inland have a tendency to call their lakes the 'sea'. Mention Dali to a Chinese person and the first thing that would come to their mind would be the Duan emperors of Dali, glorified as gongfu masters in Chinese gongfu movies and classic novels.

Dali was once the heart of a large empire set up by a confederation of Thai-related tribes led by the Bai people. The Nanchao Dali

Empire once included not only Yunnan, but also large parts of southwestern China and the northern parts of Myanmar, Laos and Vietnam. The empire, which was a largely sinified one even at its height during the later part of the Chinese Tang Dynasty — its state documents were written in Chinese — was eventually destroyed by the Mongolian invading forces. It was partially that invasion which set off the movement of the Thai tribes southwards to what is today Thailand.

Dali is a relaxed town where pretty local Bai ladies walk around in traditional costumes (along with their beloved mobile phones). I spent a few days here visiting the lake and the city's historical monuments. Tim, an American backpacker who spoke five languages (and some basic Chinese words), and I took a bus to a seldom-visited Bai village called Shiba, on its market day. Not for the first time on my journey through China did locals assume that I was a tour guide with some white tourist. When Tim showed interest in local jade, the vendors jostled to make me various offers — if Tim made a purchase, I would get a kickback of 20%. Interesting! Hmm, considering my state of (un)employment, perhaps I should have persuaded Tim to buy something.

It was definitely an advantage speaking the language. We dropped by a Bai eating place in Shiba and had tea while speaking briefly to the proprietor and her family. When we were about to leave, they not only refused payment but also invited us for lunch. "Welcome again,

The ancient pagodas of Dali, Yunnan. Yunnan is an amazing province of geographical, ethnic and architectural diversity.

guests from afar," they said. The Bai people were very friendly, and so were many members of China's ethnic minorities. They seemed a lot more relaxed and hospitable than most urban Han. My ability to speak Mandarin had enabled me to chat with these people, something I had been unable to achieve in Latin America, where I was attracted to colourful tribal costumes and traditions.

We explored the tiny Muslim quarter of Dali and came across an amazing Catholic Church, built also in traditional southern Chinese temple architectural style, topped with a cross flanked with Chinese dragons and kirins, the latter a Chinese mythological creature. The Christians of Dali, living in splendid isolation in these mountains, had constructed a house of God in the style that they were familiar with, and in line with their own cultural traditions. I loved this — too many religious purists in the world are destroying their own cultures in the name of a foreign religion. I hope the Christians of Dali will continue to preserve this in time to come, and not replace it with a Gothic structure just because some foreign Christians have given them funds.

We also visited the local mosque (yet another place not listed in *Lonely Planet*), which was also built in the traditional Chinese-style. A large memorial plaque told the tale of a local Islamic saint and his most un-Islamic sounding deeds.

This saint, a native of Gansu Province, had fallen in love with Dali during his travels, and decided to settle there. He set up the mosque and a *madrasah* (Islamic college) here to promote the teachings of the Prophet and Allah's decrees. During his free time, he often meditated in a cave nearby, where he communicated the word of Allah to tigers and dragons. One day, a black dragon appeared in Dali and the saint turned him into a giant bull hanging on a tree. On another occasion, he lifted hundreds of kilograms of giant goat liver up in the air. All these events impressed the local people and educated them on the powers of Allah, the one and only true God. After the death of the saint, his grave became a local pilgrimage site and miracles of all kinds continued to occur there, so stated the plaque. Well, impressed? *Allahu Akbar!* It sounded more paganistic than Islamic...

***

I travelled three hours northwards through the soaring mountains along yet another of China's many new expressways. These were the eastern foothills of the Himalayas, where the vertical cliffs hid many isolated valleys remote from external influences.

Lijiang, the 'beautiful river' as it was known in Chinese, also the heart of Naxi country, was my next destination. This is the most beautiful Chinese city I have ever been to (Yunnan being the 18th Chinese province on my journey). Next to a concrete new city rebuilt after the great earthquake of 1996 was the old city which survived the disaster. Just imagine an old city in a valley surrounded by mountains, flanked on one side by the gorgeous snowcapped Jade Dragon Snow Mountain. Clear, fast-flowing streams criss-crossed the old city, making it a mini-Venice of sorts. Elderly Naxi ladies in their traditional blue costumes and young priests in bright yellow headdress were singing ancient religious Dongba songs in the quaint Sifang Jie, the central square of the UNESCO-listed World Heritage city.

Dongba is the ancient religion of the Naxi people. It is a form of shamanism, with the worship of nature and the elements. Dongba's religious texts are written in a hierographic or pictographic form and found all over the old city on road signs. Well-off Naxi men walked around both the new and old cities with hunting eagles on their arms, like Parisians walking around the city with their dogs after dinner. No wonder many Chinese backpackers have fallen in love with this place and have settled here, opening small inns and restaurants in the many pretty, old Naxi houses with their square-ish courtyards and compounds.

Lijiang was crowded with tourists and yet it remained true to its traditions. Every evening, the famous Naxi scholar, Mr Xuan Ke, hosted a traditional Naxi concert here. The orchestra, comprised mainly of elderly Naxi gentlemen, some of whom were in their 80s, played old Tang Chinese music which the Naxi princes of the Mu family had acquired from the interior of China proper. Such music which had been long lost in the Han parts of China, but have been preserved in this remote frontier region by the Naxi people. This was also similar to the Nanyin music of Singapore, where the Hokkien people have preserved long-lost Tang music, although one wonders how long this will be so.

The Naxi people are also an open-minded people who have turned their homeland into a melting pot of ideas and religions. Visit the Baisha Mu family temples, and one would will find frescoes adorned with the common symbols of Dongba, Taoism, Confucianism and Tibetan Buddhism, the four religions that co-exist together in the Naxi country. The most prominent fresco portrayed Buddha, whom the Naxi believed was also a manifestation of Taoism's supreme teacher Laozhi, surrounded by Tibetan *boddhisatvas* and Taoist gods and deities in their flowing robes, and scattered in the background, symbols of the Naxi's own original Dongba faith.

***

I joined a group of seven Chinese backpackers, hired a van and a most knowledgeable and fun-loving Naxi guide, and set off for the Tiger Leaping Gorge, a spectacular gorge along the upper reaches of the Changjiang (or Yangtze), known as the Jinshajiang (Golden Sands River) at this stretch. This was a beautiful but treacherous valley that had killed a number of hikers over the years, including at least one Singaporean a few years ago. Falling rocks and slippery slopes were the main culprits, and yet they did not deter the 68-year-old granny in our group.

Up and down the cliff-sides of the Tiger Leaping Gorge we went over the next two days, passing through the pretty village of Hetaoyuan ('Walnut Grove'). We had a nice lunch at the Halfway Hostel, with an incredible view over the gorge. In fact, the toilet at Halfway, partially exposed to the open cliffs and clear blue sky, had a great view of the soaring heights and the snow-capped peaks of the Haba Snow Mountains, and is renowned in the Chinese backpacking world for having the best toilet view in the world!

We drove around the winding mountain roads of Lijiang and Diqing prefectures, visiting local markets, Alpine lakes, Naxi holy sites, as well as Tibetan and Yi villages. My favourite trick was to offer Yi tribal nannies cigarettes, have a light chat with them and then request for a photo or two. It was hard to imagine that these graceful women worked in the fields with their amazingly huge squarish head-dress, sometimes measuring up to $1m^2$ in size.

Then on to Zhongdian, a dusty, god-forsaken ethnic Tibetan town 3,000m above sea level in northwestern Yunnan, which was recently renamed Shangri-La, in line with local attempts to cash in on the Shangri-La of James Hilton's 1933 novel, *Lost Horizon*, the mysterious land of Utopia, where man lived forever. Zhongdian, with its large Tibetan monastery complex on bare hill slopes, was my first introduction to Tibetan culture. Prayer flags fluttered in the crystal-clear sky while peasants spread their grains on the roads to dry, ignoring the numerous tourist buses passing through, to that supposed Shangri-La.

The Chinese themselves have caught on to the romance of Tibet, despite the obvious political differences. A few in my Chinese backpacking group (myself being the only real foreigner) had been to Tibet and they, too, like many Westerners, have a romanticised image of the land and its people. Tibetan music and other images of Tibetan cultural symbols have become fashionable across China these days.

However, the views of even the most ardent Tibet fans among the Chinese are very different from those of the West: they see Tibet as being a part of China and that they are trying to develop Tibet, to modernise it like the rest of China. That explains why many Chinese also volunteer to be teachers, engineers or doctors in the region, doing work no different from the US Peace Corps or aid programmes elsewhere in the world, although their work is, more often than not, seen as being highly controversial to people in many other parts of the world.

What is encouraging are recent reports of increasingly high-profile talks between Beijing and the Dharam
sala. The Dalai Lama is obviously concerned about his age and the growing sinification of Tibet, and Beijing being more sophisticated in its global PR efforts. Perhaps a deal could be struck somehow. It is Xinjiang that is more worrying. A growing insurgency of some sort has appeared in parts of western Xinjiang. The nationality issue is something China has to deal with, not just through military means but also politically, for the events in Moscow have shown that pure military tactics do not resolve long-term political issues.

Whatever it is, Tibet is now on my extremely long 'to go' list. When will I ever get there?

***

Back in Kunming, I took an atrocious 21-hour bus journey from temperate China into tropical China, initially through a smooth modern highway, and then through awful old winding roads up and down the

ountains. I was told that a new highway was being built that would
duce the journey by half.

 Yes, I have finally left Northeast Asia and entered Southeast Asia.
was in Jinhong, capital of the Xishuangbanna Dai Autonomous
efecture at the southern tip of the Yunnan province. Xishuangbanna
the tropical part of China. Very hot and humid, it had the scent of
gar cane and bananas in the air. The main ethnic group there was the
ai, who wore large straw hats and colourful sarongs, and celebrated
eir new year by splashing pails of water around, like the Thais and
s. The Dai language is very close to Thai and Lao, and the
nguage is based on the Burmese script. Apart from the Dai,
he Lahu-Lahu, Yao and Hani ethnic groups. I saw many
d Buddhist monks, water buffaloes and signs warning
out the presence of wild elephants. All these indicated
ft Northeast Asia and entered Southeast Asia.

s the biggest story of the decade, possibly the century. Despite
s in Tibet and Xinjiang, China has become the alternative
ts businessmen are buying up the world, and its tourists are
turn in malls worldwide. The Beijing Olympics of 2008 has
rld with the country's organisational might and technological
hile Shanghai Expo in 2010 has the world kowtowed to China
cuberant display of what they have to offer.

Tan Wee Cheng is Singaporean and a self-confessed travel junk
who has been to over 190 countries and territories over the last tw
decades. He is listed in the 2008 *Book of Singapore Records* as th
Singaporean who has been to the most number of countri   ha
a weak spot for controversial places and a tendency to ge
troubles, such as getting arrested by corrupt police
Kyrgyzstan, Russia and the rebel state of Transdniestri.
He has survived road accidents in Albania and floo
getting mugged in Jerusalem, St. Petersburg and L
almost getting into a fight with a Cypriot gangster.

Wee Cheng has worked in the financial sector in S
UK and China, as an auditor, investment banker, finan
and as the chief financial officer of a listed company. F
an adjunct associate professor of accounting at a
Singapore. These days he spends his leisure time plannin
working on his travel website (http://weecheng.con
organise travel talks for SgTravelCafe.com travel for
endless slices of good old kaya toast.

His other book, *Hot Spots and Dodgy Places*, also a c
travel stories, was published by Marshall Cavendish in 2009.

Wee Cheng invites readers to email him at letters@weecheng..